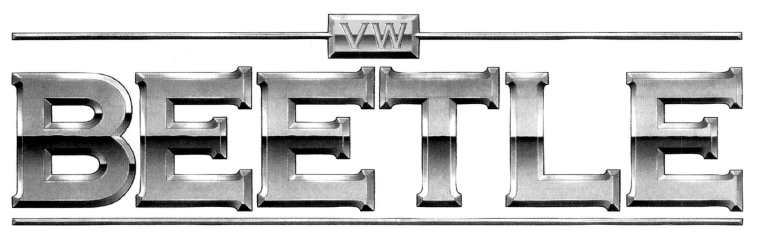

VW BEETLE

A comprehensive illustrated history of the world's most popular car

Keith Seume

Motorbooks International
Publishers & Wholesalers

This edition first published in 1997 by Motorbooks International Publishers & Wholesalers, 729 Prospect Avenue, PO Box 1, Osceola, WI 54020, USA

CLB 4457
©1997 CLB International, Godalming Business Centre, Woolsack Way, Godalming, Surrey GU7 1XW, UK

The information in this book is true and complete to the best of our knowledge. All recommendations are made without any guarantee on the part of the author or publisher, who also disclaim any liability incurred in connection with the use of this data or specific details.

We recognize that some words, model names and designations, for example, mentioned herein are the property of the trademark holder. We use them for identification purposes only. This is not an official publication.

Motorbooks International books are also available at discounts in bulk quantity for industrial or sales-promotional use. For details write to Special Sales Manager at the Publisher's address.

Library of Congress Cataloging-in-Publication Data Available.

ISBN 0-7603-0430-0

The author and publishers would like to express their thanks to Herr Eckbert von Witzleben, the archivist at the AutoMuseum Volkswagen in Wolfsburg, and his colleagues, Frau Renate Sänger, Frau M. Rettig, and Herr Roland Hendel, who were so helpful in arranging facilities for photography in the Museum and for opening the photographic archives for consultation. The majority of the historical photographs reproduced in this book were obtained from the Museum's archive, the remainder coming from the author's own collection. Thanks also to Volkswagen's Press Office in Wolfsburg and to Paul Bucket of Volkswagen UK for pictures of Concept 1 and the New Beetle.

A special expression of gratitude should also be offered to the owners of the cars who patiently sat through long days in the studio to allow us to take the photographs of the landmark cars that are featured throughout the book.

Keith Seume is a Volkswagen enthusiast of long standing, having driven his first Beetle at the age of 14. He became a motoring journalist in 1976. In 1987 he launched *Volksworld* magazine, a publication devoted to the VW Beetle, of which he is currently Consultant Editor. He is the author of several other illustrated books on the Beetle in its many guises, including *The VW Beetle Custom Handbook, VW Beetle Coachbuilts and Cabriolets, Essential VW Beetle Cabriolet, California Look VW* and *The Air-Cooled VW Interchange Manual*.

Keith became involved in building race engines for VWs in 1974 and was active in rallycross and circuit racing for the next few years. He started drag racing Volkswagens in 1988 and has succeeded in winning three class championships in his own drag racers. His current stable contains no fewer than four Beetles, including the rare Okrasa-engined 1951 model featured in this book.

Credits

Studio photography:
John Alflatt
(with the exception of pages 58-59, 62-63, 92-93: George Solomonides, and 130-131, 140-141: © Volkswagen

Editor
Philip de Ste. Croix

Designer
Roger Hyde

Index
Richard O'Neill

Production
Ruth Arthur
Sally Connolly
Neil Randles
Paul Randles
Karen Staff

Director of production
Gerald Hughes

Page make-up
M.A.T.S.

Color reproduction
Pixel Tech PTE Ltd,
Singapore

Printed and bound in Singapore
KHL Printing

CONTENTS

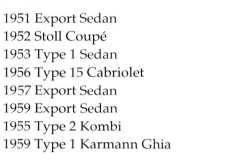

INTRODUCTION

The Volkswagen Beetle remains the world's most popular car. Against all odds, the pre-war design has survived for over fifty years to become the most successful car ever built, smashing the production record set by Ford's legendary Model T by a huge margin. That the Beetle continues to win new admirers is a testimony to the timelessness of the original Porsche-inspired concept.

The story begins back in a politically-unstable Germany of the 1930s, a country searching for an identity, a leader, a pride. With the arrival in German politics of a new figurehead by the name of Adolf Hitler, the scene was set for a major upheaval of all that had gone before. The impact of World War I had cost Germany dear, an expenditure of effort from which it would take years to recover. Gone, seemingly forever, were the days of an automobile industry dominated by luxury car manufacturers, for there was no longer a market for such vehicles. The German people, suffering from the effects of a declining economy, simply could no longer afford to buy luxury goods, let alone luxury cars.

For the man in the street, daily life meant walking or cycling to work, earning just enough money to keep his family, but little more. Some rode motorcycles, but few owned cars for they were too costly and, for most people, remained an un-attainable dream. Hitler, however, had far grander plans for his countrymen than others before him. He envisaged a German work-force which traveled everywhere by car, along

specially-built freeways, or *Autobahnen*. His vision of a car for the People – a *Volksauto*, in the popular parlance of the time – was met with a certain reticence by most people involved in the contemporary automobile industry. After all, the likes of Horch, Adler and Daimler-Benz had each founded their reputations on grand luxury cars, not on low-cost four-seater economy vehicles.

Dr. Ferdinand Porsche was one of just a few people who saw the merits of Hitler's vision as he, too, had been sketching ideas for a *Volksauto* while working with companies such as Zündapp and NSU. Hitler's proposals called for a car which could be sold for less than 1,000 Reichsmarks, a figure considered ludicrous by most industrialists, although few had the courage to take the Führer to task on the matter. For Porsche, the figure was both an absurdity and a challenge.

With Hitler's support, Porsche's project reached fruition as the *KdF-Wagen*, or Strength-Through-Joy Car, the name being taken from the Nazi KdF socialist movement. An ingenious savings scheme was announced, whereby every worker could buy stamps, the value of which eventually added up to the

cost of a new car – plus a few extras, such as compulsory insurance and delivery charges. Several thousand people signed up to join the scheme but the outbreak of World War II brought about its downfall.

The story of the Volkswagen might have ended there, in 1939, but such was the soundness of Porsche's design that the car rose, phoenix-like, from the ashes of the Wolfsburg factory where it was assembled. The tale of its rebirth is one of the great legends of automobile history, the almost derelict factory being taken over by the British Army, which viewed it as a suitable location at which to repair worn-out military vehicles. Only when some of the officers, principal among them Major Ivan Hirst of the Royal Electrical and Mechanical Engineers, saw the potential offered by the Volkswagen, as it had become known, did production recommence.

By the time the factory was handed back to the German people in 1949, the Volkswagen had proved its worth. In the hands of Heinz Nordhoff, the first post-war German head of the factory, sales of Porsche's dream car went from strength to strength. Sadly, Ferdinand Porsche himself was unable to

witness the incredible success story which followed, a story which saw every sales and production record broken, worldwide. In 1951, illness, largely brought on by a period of imprisonment in France, was to claim the life of the man without whom there would have been no Volkswagen.

The full story of the amazing car which refused to die is told here in this book – a more fantastic story could not have been dreamed up by Hollywood: a financially unstable country led by an equally unstable dictator who dreams of a car for the masses. Enter a far-sighted engineer with a team of willing employees. Mix with a world war and stir in members of the British Army. The result: a world-beater in every sense.

Since those far-off days, the Volkswagen has proved itself time and again to be one of life's great survivors. There have been many attempts to kill it off on the grounds that it was uneconomic to produce, too slow and poorly equipped for use in today's more discerning markets, or for simply not being part of the grand plan as envisaged by the heads of a modern car-manufacturing empire. But the Beetle simply refuses to lie down and die. Production continues unabated in South America and even Volkswagen's management itself has seen fit to recognize the worth of the name in marketing terms, applying the title "New Beetle" to the latest small car to roll off the production line.

Enjoy, then, the story of this world-beating car. There never will be another to take its place, for the Beetle truly is unique.

Keith Seume

Make mention of the name Porsche in most circles and the first image that comes to mind is that of an exotic sports car built in Stuttgart. Few people, outside the *cognoscenti*, ever give thought to as humble a car as the Volkswagen Beetle when talking of such a name. Yet it was the same man, Dr. Ferdinand Porsche, who was responsible for the production of both the People's Car and ultimately, through his family, such highly-desirable sports cars as the 356 and the 911.

The story begins a long, long time ago, as far back as the turn of the century, for that is when Porsche first turned his talents to car design. Born on September 3rd, 1875 at Maffersdorf, in Austria-Hungary (now known as Liberec in the Czech Republic), Ferdinand Porsche was the son of a well-respected tinsmith and soon joined his father as an apprentice to learn the skills of this worthy trade. However satisfying the prospect of carrying on the family business might have been to Ferdinand, he had his sights set far higher, for the end of the 19th century was a period when engineering technology was on the brink of expanding at an incredible rate.

Above: Ferdinand Porsche was born in 1875 at Maffersdorf, in Austro-Hungary. It was this great man who was ultimately to be responsible for the birth of the most successful car in automotive history: the Volkswagen Beetle.

The young Porsche enrolled at the local technical college in Reichensberg and studied hard, soon developing a lasting interest in two relatively new areas of technology: domestic electricity and the internal combustion engine. Having witnessed the advantages of an efficient electrical supply first hand, while visiting a nearby carpet factory, Porsche set about converting his parents' home to this new-found power source. He knew that both electricity and the combustion engine were going to prove of significant importance in the years ahead and absorbed as much information about them as he could find.

Despite his thirst for knowledge, Porsche was not an academic man in the truest sense, graduating from college with the lowest grades of his class. His brother Oskar assumed the mantle of running the family business and, with all such thoughts now firmly behind him, Porsche sought employment at Bela Egger's famous United Electrical Company at

Below: One of Porsche's first designs was this electrically-powered vehicle, the Porsche-Lohner Chaise, of 1900. It featured separate electric motors in each wheel hub – a Porsche specialty.

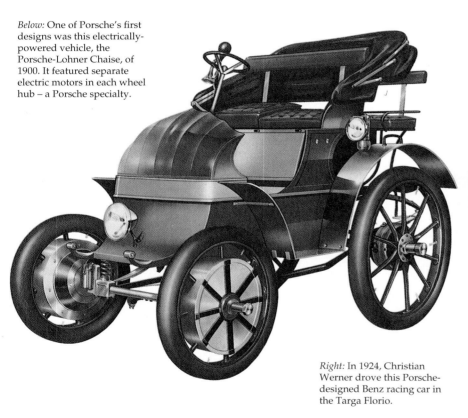

Right: In 1924, Christian Werner drove this Porsche-designed Benz racing car in the Targa Florio.

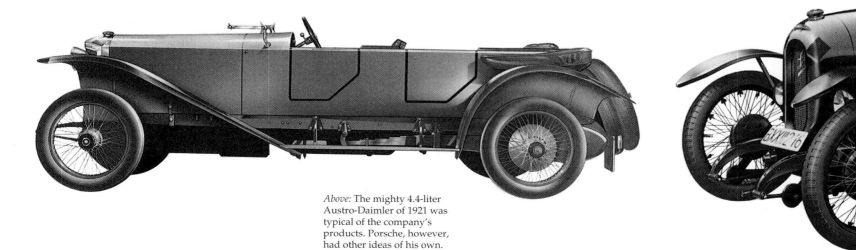

Above: The mighty 4.4-liter Austro-Daimler of 1921 was typical of the company's products. Porsche, however, had other ideas of his own.

Fernkorngasse in Vienna, where he began his career sweeping floors and acting as a maintenance technician. However, his talents were soon recognized, and after just four years he was appointed manager of the test department where he was able to experiment with some of his ideas.

Ironically, considering his poor academic grades at college, Porsche frequently sneaked secretly into lectures at the local university, where he was able to learn more about his favorite subjects. He began to sketch ideas for an electric car, a design which intrigued him, for he felt, quite rightly, that electrically-driven vehicles have much in their favor. For one thing, they are quiet and for another, they are totally without fumes. Only now, almost a century later, are many of the major car manufacturers beginning to investigate the benefits of such a concept. His first drawings were stolen, much to his fiancée Aloisia Kaes' fury, but this did not deter Ferdinand from

continuing his work. His first idea had been a highly-intriguing design, whereby each wheel of a vehicle could be powered by its own electric motor fitted within the hub. The thinking behind this somewhat radical idea was that, at the time, almost all cars suffered from poor transmission design. Power losses were simply too great, while the output and reliability of contemporary internal combustion engines left much to be desired. He developed his concept further and showed it to Ludwig Lohner, head of Jakob Lohner & Co, a well-established carriage builder in Vienna.

Lohner had himself already been investigating the possibility of offering an electrically-powered vehicle, feeling that the noisy and smelly internal combustion engine would probably not appeal to his more staid customers. However, although Lohner had a solid customer base and was an accomplished carriage builder, his company lacked the technical expertise to produce the sort of vehicle

he proposed. Porsche's designs and obvious talent were just what Lohner needed and, in 1898, he offered the young engineer a job as his designer.

Overnight Success

The result of this collaboration was the Porsche-Lohner Chaise, an electric vehicle with Porsche's beloved hub-drive motors, which proved capable of covering some 80km (50 miles) without recharging. The design so impressed Lohner that he asked Porsche to take the car to the 1900 Paris Universal Exposition where it was the subject of great interest, so much so that it was awarded a Grand Prize. At a time when motoring matters were dominating thinking, Porsche's success at the exposition made him famous overnight.

The next step was to develop a new vehicle which combined electric power with the internal combustion engine. A Daimler petrol engine was used to power generators which,

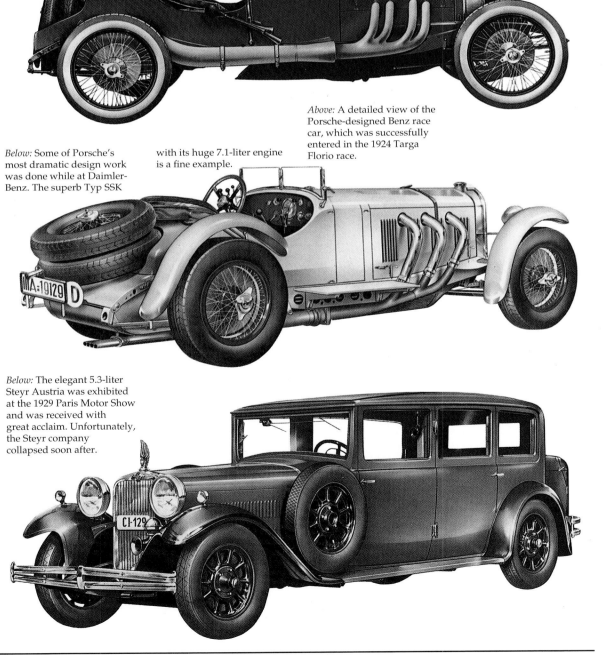

Above: A detailed view of the Porsche-designed Benz race car, which was successfully entered in the 1924 Targa Florio race.

Below: Some of Porsche's most dramatic design work was done while at Daimler-Benz. The superb Typ SSK with its huge 7.1-liter engine is a fine example.

Below: The elegant 5.3-liter Steyr Austria was exhibited at the 1929 Paris Motor Show and was received with great acclaim. Unfortunately, the Steyr company collapsed soon after.

Above: Porsche's swan-song for Austro-Daimler was the pretty little Sascha sports car. It proved to be a great success in competition.

in turn, supplied electricity to the hub-mounted motors. The car was an instant success, receiving much acclaim among many people in high society. The car, called the Mixt, proved to be popular, but it still did not satisfy Porsche – he had even more designs up his sleeve. Lohner, on the other hand, seemed quite content to concentrate on selling the Mixt, having spent a large sum of money on its development costs. Porsche became restless and when, in 1905, he received an offer of employment from Austro-Daimler (or more correctly, Oesterreichische Daimler Motoren Werke), he readily accepted.

Within a year, Porsche was promoted to technical director and appointed to the board of the rather strait-laced company which was an offshoot of Daimler in Germany. There, he developed a car by the name of the Maja, a rather more conventional vehicle with a four-cylinder gasoline engine and four-speed transmission. Even at this early stage in his professional life – Porsche was still only in his early thirties – he realized the value of success in competition as far as car sales were concerned. He entered three cars in the 1909 Prinz Heinrich endurance trial and all three won awards. The following year, Porsche entered an entirely new, streamlined car which earned itself the title of *Tulpenform,* or Tulip-shaped. Austro-Daimler cars won a total of twelve of the seventeen test stages and took the first three prizes, the lead car driven by Ferdinand Porsche himself.

Military Matters

With the threat of war in Europe looming ever larger, Porsche found himself increasingly involved with designing aero-engines for Austro-Daimler. These impressive units, each capable of producing over 300bhp yet weighing far less than their contemporary rivals, were used in both aircraft and dirigibles. In 1913, he was called upon to design a tractor unit, capable of pulling an immense mortar developed by the military. His design was based upon the principle of gasoline/electrical power first used in the Mixt car for Lohner. It almost goes without saying that the design was a success and saw regular action throughout World War I.

However, the war resulted in defeat for the German Empire and the consequent collapse of its financial fortunes. At a stroke, there was little or no demand for the fine vehicles which Porsche had been responsible for designing while employed with Lohner and Austro-Daimler. However, Porsche was not one to look on the black side. Instead he realized there would soon be a demand for an inexpensive family car, capable of fulfilling the role pioneered by Ford's legendary Model T in America. Others in his company were not so convinced, feeling that Austro-Daimler should continue to build the large, quality limousines for which it was famous. Even when

Left: The Zündapp Type 12 took to the road in April 1932. It was derived from Porsche's Project No 12 and featured torsion bar suspension with a rear-mounted engine of radial configuration. It is believed this car survived until as late as 1944, when it was apparently destroyed in an air raid on the VW factory.

Left: One of the three Type 32 prototypes built for NSU in 1934. This is one of two which featured bodywork by the Drauz *karosserie,* constructed of artificial leather over a wooden frame – popularly known as the Weymann technique.

Below: Several prototype engine designs would be tried before Porsche settled on his final choice. This early horizontally-opposed four-cylinder unit proved prone to seizing due to a lack of adequate cooling – note the absence of an oil-cooler.

the company received a commission to build a small, lightweight sports car for competition use – subsequently called the Sascha – the directors showed no enthusiasm. Again Porsche's design was a success but Austro-Daimler refused to make more funds available to develop it. Ultimately, after an explosive meeting with the company's financiers, Porsche stormed out.

The German Daimler concern was quick to make him an offer and Porsche was appointed to the position of technical director and became a member of the board at the Stuttgart factory. His blunt manner did not always go down well with the somewhat conservative Daimler management, but he soon earned the respect of his workforce. He proceeded to design a number of impressive vehicles under Daimler's prestigious Mercedes name, several of which were to become legends in their own lifetimes, such as the mighty SS and SSK models with their thundering super-charged engines.

Troubled Times

However, Porsche still longed to be able to push forward his idea for a car for the masses, but once again met with resistance from his employers. Ironically, one of the reasons why his pleas were met with indifference was that, as the economy was in decline, Daimler felt it should concentrate on building only profitable models. To Daimler, that meant large, luxury vehicles, not some small, low-cost family cars. Once again, a disagreement with management saw Porsche's departure from Stuttgart, this time following the merger of Daimler and Benz & Cie in 1926. With more than a hint of irony, the alleged cause of the disagreement was over the reliability of a new small car called the Stuttgart!

Porsche was immediately offered a position at Steyr, in Vienna, and in 1929 he found himself heading for his homeland. At Steyr, he was responsible for the design of two successful cars, a small sedan very much along the lines of Daimler's Stuttgart model, and a larger limousine, called the Austria. Both were fine vehicles and met with much acclaim, especially when displayed at the 1929 Paris Motor Show. However, Porsche's euphoria was short-lived for Steyr collapsed and the company's affairs were, coincidentally, handed over to the same financiers who handled Austro-Daimler. With his enthusiasm for car manufacturing at an all-time low, Ferdinand Porsche turned his back on further employment within the car industry and headed for Stuttgart once more to open a design studio – the Porsche Bureau – through which he could offer his services to industry as an engineering consultant. The date was January 1st, 1931.

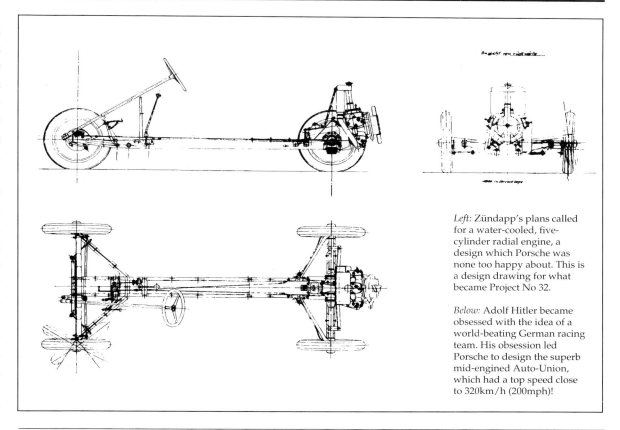

Left: Zündapp's plans called for a water-cooled, five-cylinder radial engine, a design which Porsche was none too happy about. This is a design drawing for what became Project No 32.

Below: Adolf Hitler became obsessed with the idea of a world-beating German racing team. His obsession led Porsche to design the superb mid-engined Auto-Union, which had a top speed close to 320km/h (200mph)!

Following his first attempts at building a *Volksauto*, or People's Car, in association with the Zündapp motorcycle company, Ferdinand Porsche embarked on a new project with Fritz von Falkenhayn of the successful NSU organization. The result, in 1934, of this collaboration was Project No 32: an aerodynamic saloon powered by an air-cooled, horizontally opposed four-cylinder engine. The chosen suspension medium was Porsche's beloved torsion bar. A total of three examples were built, of which just one survives in the AutoMuseum at Wolfsburg. This is the oldest surviving vehicle which can be considered a true Volkswagen prototype.

SPECIFICATIONS

Engine: Horizontally opposed, air-cooled four cylinder. **Construction:** Two-piece cast-alloy crankcase split vertically with separate cast-iron cylinders and cast aluminum alloy pistons. Four main bearings. Cast aluminum cylinder heads with individual inlet ports. **Bore and stroke:** 80mm x 73mm. **Capacity:** 1467cc (89.5ci). **Valves:** Pushrod operated overhead. **Compression ratio:** n/a. **Fuel system:** Mechanical fuel pump; single Solex carburetor. **Maximum power:** 28bhp (32 US hp) at 3,300rpm. **Maximum torque:** n/a

Transmission: Four-speed manual, non-synchromesh transaxle with integral final drive unit. Two-piece casing. **Gear ratios:** n/a

Brakes: Cable-operated drums on all four wheels

Steering: Worm and nut

Suspension: Front: Fully independent with transverse torsion bars and telescopic dampers. King- and link-pin design. **Rear:** Fully independent swing-axle with twin torsion bars and lever arm dampers.

Wheels and tires: 4J x 16in pressed steel wheels. 5.20 x 16 cross-ply tires.

Dimensions: Length: n/a. **Width:** n/a. **Height:** n/a. **Wheelbase:** 2400mm (7ft 10.5in). **Dry weight:** 790kg (1742lb).

Peformance: Maximum speed: 90km/h (55mph). **Acceleration:** 0-96km/h (60mph): n/a. **Fuel consumption:** n/a.

Number built: (1934) 3

Owner: Volkswagen AG

Left: The engine was a horizontally opposed, air-cooled flat four, like that of the Beetle, but with a capacity of 1467cc. The power output was a modest 32hp which allowed the Type 32 to reach a maximum speed of 90km/h (56mph).

Above: The dashboard was unique to the model, featuring an octagonal speedometer and scattered minor controls. The emergency (hand) brake was situated beneath the dashboard and may be seen below the speedometer.

Below: In this profile view of the sole-surviving NSU prototype, it is possible to make out the familiar lines of the Beetle. From the very beginning, Porsche preferred the idea of an aerodynamic, rear-engined vehicle to the more traditional upright designs of the period.

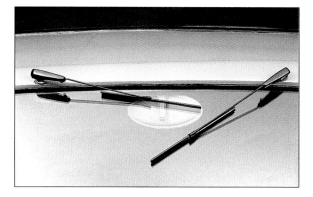

Right: From the front, the snub-nosed Type 32 displays its low-set headlamps mounted in separate front fenders. Porsche incorporated pressed moldings in the front panel to provide extra strength. Note the slit-like rear windshield.

Below: A number of headlamp configurations were tried. The units shown here are not the originals.

Above: Unlike the production models of the future, the windshield wipers of the 1932 prototype were located at the top of the windshield and swept outwards. The oval-shaped interior mirror is similar to those fitted to the first Beetles.

Left: Interior trim was simple in the extreme, with coarse cloth being used as the covering for door and side trim panels.

Above: The vents behind the rear side windows were to allow air to the engine. This is one feature which did not make it into production.

Torsion Bars

The new bureau's first client was the Wanderer Auto Company, for whom Porsche designed a pair of cars, neither being the "People's Car" which he so longed to build. However, he did incorporate at least one design idea which he had been considering for some time: torsion bar suspension. Porsche had long felt that the days of the traditional leaf spring were numbered, especially since it was very difficult to achieve the correct spring rate, and hence an acceptable ride quality, when using such a suspension medium on a lightweight vehicle. Porsche's torsion system consisted of a bar, one end of which was held solidly in the chassis, the other end being connected to the wheels and allowed to twist as the suspension rose and fell over rough ground. There were two major advantages to this design: torsion bar suspension is very compact (and thus lends itself to use on a small car) and it displays a rising spring rate,

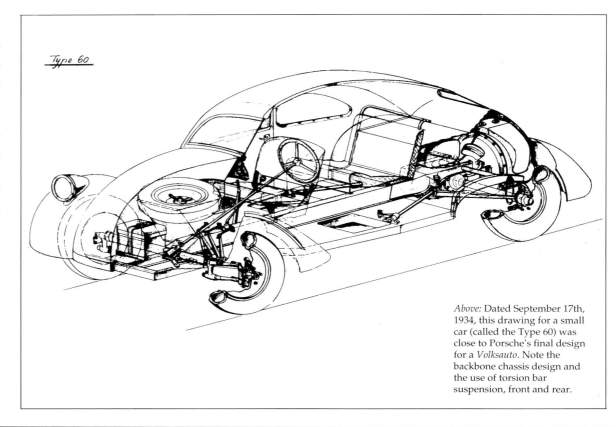

Type 60

Above: Dated September 17th, 1934, this drawing for a small car (called the Type 60) was close to Porsche's final design for a *Volksauto*. Note the backbone chassis design and the use of torsion bar suspension, front and rear.

Left: The aluminum-bodied V2 cabriolet was extensively tested with the V1 sedan. In the foreground, Ferdinand Porsche (right, with back to camera) is in discussion with his son, Ferry.

Right: Thirty VW30 models were test-driven for over 80,000km (50,000 miles) by a team of army personnel. Powered by a 985cc air-cooled engine, the VW30 proved a rugged design.

Below: Outside Porsche's house in Stuttgart, a VW30 prototype (left) rests alongside an earlier VW3 sedan. Note how similar the two designs appeared to be.

i.e., the more the suspension is deflected, the stiffer it becomes.

So, some of the elements of the future Beetle were starting to come together: a downturn in the German economy, Porsche's long-held dream for a small car and now the ideal suspension system. What was missing was a company prepared to give Porsche his head. A tempting offer was to come from an unlikely source.

In 1932, Ferdinand was approached by a Soviet delegation, who wished to offer him the opportunity to emigrate to the USSR and become an industrial designer. The offer was extremely tempting, for the Soviets offered Porsche everything he could want, including a new home for his wife and family, a blank check and the possibility of starting work on a small car for the masses. However, despite a visit to the USSR which left him very impressed, Porsche felt that he could not bring himself to turn his back on his homeland and

the team he had built up around him.

Returning to his design bureau, Porsche soon found himself in contact with Fritz Neumeyer, head of the Zündapp motorcycle company. Neumeyer, like Porsche, believed that the time was right for the introduction of a small car – a *kleinauto* – which would appeal to the person who wished to progress from riding a motorcycle to owning a family car. Indeed, Zündapp had even been sketching some ideas of its own.

Project No 12

For Ferdinand Porsche, the whole concept of a car for the people had become something of an obsession. He devoted much time and effort, and his own money, to designing a small car of revolutionary layout. The design, known as Project No 12, was a strange looking vehicle with a sloping nose, curved rear bodywork and a rear-mounted engine. The reason for the latter configuration was to provide

better traction on indifferent road surfaces, something that may have been a problem due to the vehicle's low weight. Naturally, Porsche's beloved torsion bar suspension was also part of the plan.

Perhaps the most technically intriguing part of the design was the engine itself: a peculiar three-cylinder unit with the cylinders mounted radially about the crankshaft, rather like an aircraft engine. Air-cooling helped keep both the cost and the weight to a minimum. Also worthy of note was the lack of a conventional chassis. Porsche's work on aircraft design had led him to appreciate the quite considerable weight benefits that could be had by careful strengthening of what might otherwise appear to be a rather weak design. A flat, sheet metal pan with a central backbone member was made more rigid by the clever use of small, but effective, ribs pressed into the metalwork.

After three months devoted to perfecting

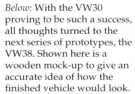

Right: The test route for the VW30s took them up into the mountains where their air-cooled engines excelled. At the time, the radiators of most water-cooled vehicles would boil over when pushed to such limits.

Below: With the VW30 proving to be such a success, all thoughts turned to the next series of prototypes, the VW38. Shown here is a wooden mock-up to give an accurate idea of how the finished vehicle would look.

the design on paper, Porsche was forced to consider putting the whole project on hold as he was fast running out of money. However, despite the indifference shown by others in the industry to Project No 12, Fritz Neumeyer heard of the design, asked to see the drawings and liked what he saw. Porsche was given the go-ahead to develop the concept as far as building three running prototypes. However, there was to be one major alteration: the engine should be a five-cylinder, water-cooled design of radial layout. Porsche was not enthusiastic but agreed to make the change. It was to prove a mistake as these first cars were terribly unreliable, their engines seizing almost immediately. To add to the problem, Porsche's suspension system proved troublesome, with the torsion bars snapping with frustrating regularity.

Neumeyer became downhearted with the whole situation and rapidly lost interest, preferring instead to concentrate on building

motorcycles. Porsche was thanked for his efforts, paid a sum of money and given one of the prototypes to take away. It is worth noting that this car continued in regular use until 1944, when it is believed to have been destroyed in an air-raid on the factory. Needless to say, Porsche was disappointed at

the outcome of Project No 12. It was a classic case of so-near-yet-so-far.

However, hope was in sight when Fritz von Falkenhayn, head of the NSU company, let it be known that his company was interested in developing a *Volksauto*, or People's Car. Porsche once more rose to the challenge and produced a prototype – Project No 32. This was similar to its Zündapp predecessor, but more refined in its overall appearance. The headlamps, for example, were incorporated into the front fenders and the whole body shape was more graceful. The greatest improvement, as far as Porsche was concerned, was the adoption of an air-cooled engine, this time a four-cylinder, horizontally-opposed design, not unlike the aero engines he had designed for Austro-Daimler.

A total of three prototypes were built and each proved to be a success, despite continuing problems with the torsion bar suspension. The cause of the breakages was discovered to

Above: The addition of an oil-cooler finally solved all over-heating problems. However, the design of the cylinder head had still not been decided upon when this VW30 engine was built.

Left: The torsion bar suspension was one of the secrets of the project's success. Compact in design, the system was perfectly suited for use in a small car.

Above: The VW38 series of prototypes was extensively tested over all kinds of terrain. Two examples, one a cabriolet, the other a sedan are shown here at the Stelvio Pass in the Italian Alps, accompanied by an earlier VW2 cabrio (center).

Left: Ferdinand Porsche surveys his brainchild. The three variations, cabriolet, sun-roof sedan and regular sedan, receive a final check-over at Porsche workshops. At last, Porsche's dream had been all but realized – the People's Car was no longer simply a vision.

be a matter of incorrect heat treatment of the metal, not one of a flawed basic concept. Von Falkenhayn was delighted with the cars, being especially impressed by the performance, and gave his approval to further development of the *Volksauto*.

The Rise of Hitler

However, history was about to be made in German political circles when, on January 30th, 1933, an ambitious Adolf Hitler was appointed Chancellor of Germany by von Hindenburg, the President. Hitler, head of the German National Socialist Workers' (or Nazi) party, was an unashamed car enthusiast. Indeed, ten years earlier he had spent the last of his party's funds on buying himself an expensive Mercedes-Benz for "official purposes." His first official engagement was to open the 1933 Berlin Motor Show, where he took the opportunity to speak out about his grand plan to motorize Germany, building a network of motorways – or *autobahnen* – along which the German people could travel in their very own cars. Quite what inspired Hitler to have this vision is unclear – his own love was for powerful, high-performance cars, even though he never himself learned to drive a vehicle. Possibly the idea came to him while he was in prison, some ten years earlier, where he read a copy of Henry Ford's autobiography. Ford's writings captivated the young Hitler, with their tales of mass production and cheap motoring – or maybe it was simply the fact that Ford was known to hold anti-Semitic views that appealed to Hitler's imagination.

Whatever the reason behind it, Hitler's speech sent shock waves through the German car industry, for few of the larger, well-established manufacturers had shown any interest in a *Volksauto*, as Porsche was only too well aware. At the time, he was working with NSU on Project No 32, and also with Auto-Union on the design of a radical new racing car, intended to take on the might of Mercedes-Benz on the race tracks of Europe. As Mercedes had been given a government subsidy by Hitler, Porsche argued that Auto-Union deserved the same. Hitler disagreed, feeling that Germany only needed one outstanding car in order to beat foreign rivals. Porsche argued long and hard, laying out the proposed technical specification of the Auto-Union: a mid-mounted, V-16 engine, torsion bar suspension with trailing arms at the front, swing-axles at the rear, and an impressive streamlined body. By the end of his outburst, Porsche had convinced Hitler of his argument and a subsidy was made available to Auto-Union. The result was a series of race cars which not only beat the Mercedes-Benz team cars on a regular basis, but also dominated Grand Prix racing in Europe. They were

Above: The estate of Count von Schulenburg, Schloss Wolfsburg, at Fallersleben, was the site chosen for the new factory. The Count had little to say in the matter as the location was chosen for its proximity to the Mittelland Canal.

Right: Peter Koller, seen here to the left of center in the photograph, was chosen as the architect responsible for designing the new city. Adolf Hitler and Ferdinand Porsche admire the model of his proposed design.

Below: Koller's designs included accommodation for the workers and extensive leisure facilities. The large building to the right would become the Luigi Cianetti Hall, named after the Italian Minister of Labor, which could accommodate up to 5,000 people at a time.

By the end of the 1930s, Porsche was at last able to prove to himself that the concept of a People's Car was a sound one. Following extensive testing of the prototype VW38 cars, of which a series of 44 was built, the full go-ahead was given for the production of the KdF-Wagen. Unfortunately, the onset of war effectively brought the KdF project to a halt, at least as far as the general public was concerned. This VW38, which bears the chassis number 3803, is the last survivor of the original pre-production prototypes and can be seen in the Auto-Museum at Wolfsburg. At last, the familiar Beetle shape had been established. It was indeed the beginning of a legend.

Above: The dashboard layout of the VW38 was simple but attractive, with two open glove boxes and a pair of central panels, one of which housed the speedometer – the second panel displayed a diagram of the gear shift pattern. This dashboard layout would remain fundamentally unchanged until 1953.

Left: The small oval-shaped mirror was similar to that used on the first production models, as was the three-point fixing.

Above: The interior light was located above and between the two split rear windows. Note the lack of headlining around the glass, which did little to help reduce noise levels inside the vehicle.

Above: The familiar lines were finalized with the last of the pre-war prototypes. Note the absence of any superfluous adornment – this was a vehicle being built down to what Porsche believed was an unrealistically low price. Every saving helped.

Right: Trim remained simple, with plain door panels being uncluttered except for the functional handles to operate the windows and open the doors.

Above: It is not difficult to see why these were frequently referred to as "banana" bumper guards. This design was superseded in 1949.

Above left & right: The rear of the VW38 has a slightly more rounded style than later production models, but is essentially the same. Note the air intake louvers under the rear windows. The front view shows the single externally-mounted horn, the simple blade bumpers and the so-called "banana" curved bumper guards.

Above: The engine produced 30hp from its 985cc at a lowly 3,000rpm. This allowed the vehicle to reach a maximum cruising speed of 97km/h (60mph). The unit proved to be extremely reliable and saw service for a further eight years.

SPECIFICATIONS

Engine: Horizontally opposed, air-cooled four cylinder. **Construction:** Two-piece cast magnesium-alloy crankcase split vertically with separate cast-iron cylinders and cast aluminum alloy pistons. Four main bearings. Cast aluminum cylinder heads with siamesed inlet ports. **Bore and stroke:** 70mm x 64mm. **Capacity:** 985cc (42ci). **Valves:** Pushrod operated overhead. **Compression ratio:** n/a. **Fuel system:** Mechanical fuel pump; single Solex carburetor. **Maximum power:** 24bhp (30 US hp) at 3,000rpm. **Maximum torque:** n/a.

Transmission: Four-speed manual, non-synchromesh transaxle with integral final drive unit. Two-piece casing. **Gear ratios:** First – 3.60; second – 2.07; third – 1.25; fourth – 0.80; reverse – 6.60. **Final drive ratio:** 4.43:1.

Brakes: Cable-operated drums on all four wheels

Steering: Worm and nut

Suspension: Front: Fully independent with transverse, multi-leaf torsion bars and telescopic dampers. King- and link-pin design. **Rear:** Fully independent swing-axle with twin solid torsion bars and lever arm dampers.

Wheels and tires: 4J x 16in pressed steel wheels. 4.25 x 16 cross-ply tires.

Dimensions: Length: 4070mm (13ft 4.2in). **Width:** 1540mm (5ft 0.6in). **Height:** 1500mm (4ft 11in). **Wheelbase:** 2400mm (7ft 10.5in). **Dry weight:** 780kg (1720lb).

Peformance: Maximum speed: 97km/h (60mph). **Acceleration:** 0-96km/h (60mph): n/a **Fuel consumption:** n/a.

Number built: (1938) 44

Owner: Volkswagen AG

reputed to be capable of speeds close to 322km/h (200mph) in a straight line.

Towards the end of the year, von Falkenhayn was forced to pull out of the *Volksauto* project, largely due to a long-standing agreement between NSU and Fiat which forbade NSU from becoming involved with car manufacture. Porsche was devastated by the news, for it must have seemed to him that he would never find a supporter for his much-loved concept. However, a chance meeting with Jakob Werlin, a Berlin Mercedes-Benz dealer and close confidant of Hitler, gave him the opportunity to discuss his plans once again. Werlin listened to Porsche with interest, knowing full well that Hitler was anxious to see such a car take to the roads. Porsche had already composed a lengthy paper on the subject and sent it to the German transport ministry, and it is almost certain that Hitler, being such a car enthusiast, would have heard of its existence.

Above: Adolf Hitler was delighted by the prospect of his People's Car finally going into production and showed great interest in the project. Here, Ferdinand Porsche explains the finer details to a smiling *Führer*.

Left: The date: May 26th, 1938. The occasion: the cornerstone-laying ceremony which marked the official birth of the new factory. Hitler examines a VW38.

Below: The occasion was full of pomp and ceremony. In his welcoming speech, Hitler referred to the new car, not as the Volkswagen, but as the KdF-Wagen – the Strength Through Joy car.

Above: The stars of the occasion were undoubtedly the three VW38 models which were on display.

In January 1934, Hitler once again addressed the crowds at the Berlin Motor Show, talking further of his wish for a car for the people – the difference this year was that by now he had been appointed Führer (leader) of the Nazi party and his words had far more political clout than they had twelve months earlier. Shortly afterwards, he asked to meet Ferdinand Porsche to discuss their individual ideas. They found they had much in common, not only in terms of car-related topics, but also in their background, for Hitler had also been born in the backwoods of Austro-Hungary. The two discussed at length their ideas for a small car, Hitler listening intently to Porsche's plans. These called for a car that weighed approximately 650kg (1,435lb), could travel at 100km/h (62mph) and used an air-cooled engine capable of producing around 26 horse-power. Hitler agreed that the engine should be air-cooled, but added that the car should be able to travel 100km for every seven liters of fuel (40mpg) and cruise at, not just reach, a speed of 100km/h (62mph). On the subject of cost, Porsche felt at this early stage that such a car could be built for around RM (Reichsmark) 1,550.

The Volksauto

Hitler was excited about the project and ordered the RDA (*Reichsverband der Deutschen Automobilindustrie*, or German motor industry association) to proceed with the scheme. The RDA was to work with Porsche and a contract was drawn up which held two surprises for the designer: the time allocated to build three prototypes was to be ten months, not one year as Porsche had initially hoped, and the cost would be no more than RM900! Porsche thought Hitler must be mad on both accounts, but looked upon the whole thing as a challenge that he would try to meet. The RDA called on the rest of the car industry to become involved with the project, but there was little enthusiasm for the scheme. Most thought it impractical, while others resented the involvement of Porsche, evidently jealous of his seemingly close relationship with Hitler. If the truth be known, the relationship extended no further than a common love of the concept of a *Volksauto* – Porsche had no political aspirations and never showed any enthusiasm for Nazi principles.

As there was little support from the rest of the industry, Porsche took it upon himself and his team to build the *Volksauto* prototypes at his Stuttgart garage. After ten months of hard work, the vehicles were still not ready and, at the 1935 Berlin Motor Show, Hitler was forced to make a speech that was, to those in the know, an exercise in stalling for time. He promised testing of the prototypes by mid-year, although Porsche knew this would not be possible. However, Hitler was not one to lose face and he remained up-beat and confident about the whole project.

Below: After the speeches, Hitler and Ferdinand Porsche were driven away in the VW38 cabriolet.

Right: Many high-ranking officials were given KdF-Wagens to drive, including labor minister, Robert Ley.

1938 VW38 CABRIOLET

From the very beginning, a cabriolet version of the People's Car had been envisaged. Indeed, the early "V" series of prototypes, built in 1935, had included a cabriolet, designated the V2. The example shown is the earliest survivor and carries the chassis number 31. Soundly constructed, the VW38 cabriolet shared the same chassis and running gear as the contemporary sedan model and proved to be very popular among the high-ranking officialdom of the time. Several photographs exist of Adolf Hitler and Hermann Goering showing great interest in the VW38 cabriolet and Hitler rode in one at the factory cornerstone-laying ceremony in May 1938.

Above: Mechanically, the 1938 cabriolet was identical to its sedan stablemate, with a 985cc engine and non-synchromesh, four-speed transmission. Note the simple "mushroom" air-filter fitted to the tiny Solex carburetor. The cooling fan and generator were driven from the crankshaft by a single belt. If this broke, the engine would quickly overheat and soon seize.

Above: The semaphore turn signals were mounted externally. On the first post-war production versions, they were mounted in the quarter-panel itself.

Above: The dashboard of the cabriolet was essentially the same as that of the sedan. The white switch at the top of the dashboard operates the turn signals.

Left: The emergency (hand) brake is located between the front seats and actuates all four drum brakes by way of a rod linkage. Ahead of the brake lever can be seen the gearshift lever.

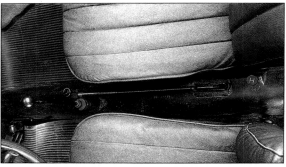
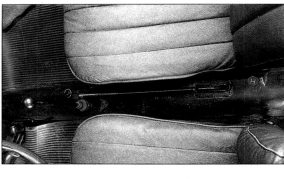
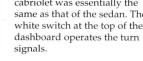

SPECIFICATIONS

Engine: Horizontally opposed, air-cooled four cylinder. **Construction:** Two-piece cast magnesium-alloy crankcase split vertically with separate cast-iron cylinders and cast aluminum alloy pistons. Four main bearings. Cast aluminum cylinder heads with siamesed inlet ports. **Bore and stroke:** 70mm x 64mm. **Capacity:** 985cc (42ci). **Valves:** Pushrod operated overhead. **Compression ratio:** n/a. **Fuel system:** Mechanical fuel pump; single Solex carburetor. **Maximum power:** 24bhp (30 US hp) at 3,000rpm. **Maximum torque:** n/a.

Transmission: Four-speed manual, non-synchromesh transaxle with integral final drive unit. Two-piece casing. **Gear ratios:** First – 3.60; second – 2.07; third – 1.25; fourth – 0.80; reverse – 6.60. **Final drive ratio:** 4.43:1.

Brakes: Cable-operated drums on all four wheels

Steering: Worm and nut

Suspension: Front: Fully independent with transverse, multi-leaf torsion bars and telescopic dampers. King- and link-pin design. **Rear:** Fully independent swing-axle with twin solid torsion bars and lever arm dampers.

Wheels and tires: 4J x 16in pressed steel wheels. 4.25 x 16 cross-ply tires.

Dimensions: Length: 4070mm (13ft 4.2in). **Width:** 1540mm (5ft 0.6in). **Height:** 1500mm (4ft 11in). **Wheelbase:** 2400mm (7ft 10.5in). **Dry weight:** 780kg (1720lb).

Peformance: Maximum speed: 97km/h (60mph). **Acceleration:** 0-96km/h (60mph): n/a. **Fuel consumption:** n/a.

Number built: (1938) n/a

Owner: Volkswagen AG

Above: The doors differed from those of the sedan in that there was no fixed window surround. Instead, the frame rose and fell with the window itself.

Above: The overall styling of the VW38 cabriolet prototype was very elegant, especially with the well-made top folded down. This sole-surviving example now resides in the AutoMuseum at Wolfsburg.

Left: So that the driver could see over the obstacle of the top when it was folded down, the driving mirror was designed to hinge up or down. It is shown here in the lower position.

Above left & right: From the front, the revised shape of the windshield surround is evident. The flatter shape was adopted for greater strength. At the rear, note the air-intake louvers are still in the main bodywork below the rear window. Post-war models would have them punched into the deck lid where they proved more efficient when the top was folded down.

Above: Wedges in the rear edge of the doors prevented flexing, by locating in cut-outs in the door pillar.

By the end of the year two prototypes were completed, but Porsche requested permission to build a third, the request being granted now that it was realized that the original timetable had been unworkable. The first two prototypes, one a sedan (V1), the other a convertible (V2), featured aluminium bodies formed over a wooden frame, while another series of three cars of the same design (VW3) were all sedans with steel bodies. As far as the engine was concerned, Porsche favored the idea of using a two-stroke design, as it was both efficient and inexpensive to build. However, testing soon showed that the design was unsuited to the chosen purpose and he finally settled on a four-cylinder, horizontally-opposed, four-stroke 985cc unit designed by Franz Reimspeiss.

The matter of cost remained a bugbear for Porsche and, indeed, for the rest of the industry. The manufacturer Opel was so sure that the project was doomed to failure that its leader, Wilhelm von Opel, suggested to Porsche that he had worked things rather nicely to his own advantage: "It's a wonderful contract, Herr Porsche. Ten months on good pay and then you tell your leaders their project is impossible." The head of BMW considered the whole idea of an inexpensive car a waste of time, suggesting with patrician hauteur that the working classes would be perfectly happy to travel everywhere by bus!

Testing Times

Also concerned about how the final product could be put into full-scale production, Porsche visited manufacturing plants in the USA to see for himself how the latest mass-production techniques could be employed in Germany. He was impressed by what he saw there, but less so when he visited the Austin factory, at Longbridge, in England. There, he felt, the factory was old and inefficient, with the production lines working at a snail's pace compared with their American counterparts.

It was not until October 12th, 1936, that the three VW Series 3 (or VW3) prototypes were eventually turned over to the RDA for testing, well over eighteen months late. The first two cars had already been driven extensively by the Porsche team, one car having covered 800km (500 miles), the second almost 4,800km (3,000 miles). The third car was delivered directly to the RDA. The cars were immediately subjected to a rigorous test schedule, which called for them to cover a total of 48,000km (30,000 miles) each, on all kinds of roads under all weather conditions. They were to be driven for 800km (500 miles) a day, six days a week until the test program was complete.

As the cars had been assembled under less than perfect conditions, with little or no

Above: At the 1938 Berlin Motor Show, Hitler examined the chassis of the new vehicle. Soon, he would be able to be driven in one – he never learned to drive.

Left: Ferdinand Porsche often visited the KdF-Wagen factory in 1938 to check on the progress being made.

Below: Adolf Hitler paid an official visit to the works on June 7th, 1939. In the background (through the windshield) can be seen Dr. Joseph Goebbels, Germany's propaganda minister.

opportunity to test materials or achieve accurate machining tolerances, failures of some kind had to be expected. Indeed, there were several members of the RDA who must have secretly hoped the whole project would prove to be abortive. Under the watchful eye of Wilhelm Vorwig, the RDA's project manager, the test program went ahead in earnest and it was not long before teething troubles made their presence felt.

One car suffered problems with the front wheel bearings, burned out its valves and then suffered brake failure on two occasions. All three cars suffered from broken crankshafts so regularly that the stock of spares was soon used up. Daimler-Benz cast some more but they too broke. It was only when replacement crankshafts were forged that the problem was effectively solved.

The final outcome of this program was a report, penned by Vorwig, which pronounced the basic design to be sound. Despite his association with the RDA, and therefore almost rival sympathies, Vorwig was forced to concede that there were few flaws in the overall concept. The many failures that had been experienced during the test period could be attributed to the fact that the cars had been built under less than favorable conditions, using materials that were frequently of imperfect quality. No part of the report, other than the matter of price, struck a negative chord as far as Hitler was concerned – the RDA was still of the opinion that the car could not be built as cheaply as the Führer had hoped.

The go-ahead was given to build a further series of thirty prototypes (VW30) which were to be test driven by some 200 army drivers, accompanied by uniformed SS officers to keep an eye on things. The extensive test schedule called for each car to cover 80,000km (50,000 miles), with the drivers showing no mercy. Indeed, the army personnel had been chosen specifically, as their lack of mechanical sympathy was most likely to imitate that of the average German worker who had probably never even driven a car before. The cars passed this new test with flying colors, although the maximum speed of 100km/h (62mph) proved to be a little difficult to attain at times. Only when an alternative 1131cc prototype engine was tried did the performance significantly improve.

A further series of 44 cars – the VW38 – was built in 1937, with several detail changes made to the design and engine construction to take into account the lessons learnt by the VW30 test program. The new car was virtually identical to the eventual production version and included such additions as a pair of D-shaped rear windows (previous prototypes had none), front-hinged doors as opposed to rear-hinged "suicide" doors and running-boards between the front and rear fenders. Mechanically, the VW38 used the 985cc engine seen in the VW30, which produced 24hp and

Left: One of the VW38s takes a rest alongside the lake at Zell-am-See in the winter of 1938/39. The cars were tested on all kinds of road and in all weather conditions.

Right: The world's motoring press was invited to drive the new car and most of the journalists returned home impressed with what they found. The test route included the new autobahn.

Below: Hitler's dream had been to build a car which was within the reach of the working man. When most Germans could barely afford to buy a motorcycle, the dream must have seemed too good to be true.

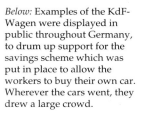

17. FEBRUAR BIS 5. MÄRZ

INTERNATIONALE AUTOMOBIL-
UND MOTORRAD-AUSSTELLUNG
BERLIN 1939

KLOKIEN

Mit K.d.F. zur
Automobilausstellung

Erkundigen Sie sich
über
KdF-SONDERZÜGE
sofort
bei Ihrem KdF-Wart
bzw.
Ihrer KdF-Dienststelle

Left: The 1939 Berlin Motor Show saw the official public launch of the KdF-Wagen. A commemorative postage stamp was even printed to celebrate the occasion, one of three depicting landmarks in German transport history.

Below: Examples of the KdF-Wagen were displayed in public throughout Germany, to drum up support for the savings scheme which was put in place to allow the workers to buy their own car. Wherever the cars went, they drew a large crowd.

had a bore and stroke of 70mm x 64mm (2.75 x 2.52in). The four-speed transmission was of a transaxle design, whereby the final drive unit was incorporated within the same casing as the gear cluster itself. With Porsche's beloved torsion bar suspension, the car had a kerb weight of 750kg (1,654lb), some 100kg (220lb) more than had originally been hoped. However, despite this weight gain, the VW38, and its immediate pre-production successor the VW39, were capable of reaching – and maintaining – a cruising speed of 100km/h (62mph).

The matter of how and where the new car – by now referred to by everybody as the *Volkswagen* or People's Car – would be produced had remained as much a mystery to

Porsche as it did to most others involved in the project. It became obvious that there could be only one satisfactory solution and that was to build a new factory from the ground up on what is known today as a "green field site." A search was made to find the ideal location; it should be near a canal or river to allow the easy transport of raw materials, and close to a source of labour. Eventually the 14th century estate of Count von Schulenburg, Schloss Wolfsburg at Fallersleben, was chosen, although it has to be said that the Count had very little say in the matter. Von Schulenburg was outraged at the idea of having to hand over a proportion of his land and protested at the highest level, but to no avail. Unfortunately, because of the proximity of the

Mittelland Canal to this estate, the Fallersleben site seemed perfect.

KdF-Stadt

Hitler appointed a young architect, by the name of Peter Koller, to design the new factory and its construction was overseen by Robert Ley, chief of the Nazi Party Labor Organization. Heeding lessons learned during Porsche's visits to the USA (a second had been made largely in an effort to tempt expatriate German technicians to return to their homeland), the new factory was built to the highest standards and followed the latest designs employed by the leading American manufacturers of the time.

On May 26th, 1938, the cornerstone of the

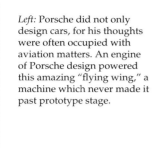

Left: Porsche did not only design cars, for his thoughts were often occupied with aviation matters. An engine of Porsche design powered this amazing "flying wing," a machine which never made it past prototype stage.

Right: For RM5 a week, workers could save for their own car. The cover of the pre-war brochure showed a *Sparkarte* savings card and the promised KdF-Wagen.

new factory was laid as part of a grand ceremony, in which Adolf Hitler made an impressive speech outlining his plans for the future. In it he referred to the new car not as the *Volkswagen* but as the *KdF-Wagen* – literally the Strength Through Joy car. The KdF (*Kraft durch Freude*) movement was his brain-child, conceived to motivate the German people by giving them a sense of purpose, promising them cheap housing, vacations and, of course, low-cost motoring. The new town built to provide housing for the work force would be called the KdF-Stadt. He also announced a revolutionary plan to allow the low-paid workers to buy their own KdF-Wagen…

This scheme was clever, of that there is no doubt, for it offered potential customers the opportunity to buy weekly savings stamps at RM5 each. A total of 50 stamps filled each book and the total cost of each car was set at RM990. However, on top of this was a RM50 delivery charge and RM200 for a two-year compulsory insurance scheme. Considering that the average worker's wage was little more than RM200-300 per month, the car was not quite the bargain it may have first seemed. Despite that, no fewer than 336,638 people signed up for the scheme, providing the government with no less than RM268 million income.

Naturally, this savings card (*Sparkarte*) scheme was like a gift from God as far as the KdF program was concerned, for not only did it provide money upfront for the whole pro-

ject, but it also amounted to the best possible market research anyone could wish for. For example, there were three different versions of the KdF-Wagen on offer: a regular sedan, a sun-roof model and a cabriolet. When they opened their savings accounts, the workers had to state which model they wanted, this form of subscription naturally giving the factory a clear indication of how many of each it would need to build. It is interesting to note that the majority of people chose to pay the extra RM60 for the optional sun-roof model. What is more distressing is that not one of those 336,638 people ever took delivery of their KdF-Wagen under the savings scheme. The outbreak of World War II in September 1939 would see to that.

As far back as 1938, there were moves afoot to produce a military version of what became known as the KdF-Wagen. In fact, early in January of that year, the head of the SS test team, Hauptsturmführer Liese, received a directive that a military version of the VW30 prototype should be prepared, to see if there was any future for such a car. Working to strict guide-lines laid down by the Wehrmacht, which called for all military vehicles to have a minimum power output of 25bhp (31hp SAE), to weigh no more than 950kg (2,094lb), including 400kg (882lb) for men and weaponry, and have a ground clearance of at least 240mm (9.5in), Porsche began to investigate the suitability of his People's Car to military use.

Starting with little more than a basic sedan, the first tests began as early as January 20th, 1938, with balloon tires providing the necessary off-road traction and increased ground clearance. A number of alternative designs were tried, including what amounted to a bare chassis fitted with flat-panelled bodywork and just two seats. The lack of ground clearance made this early prototype ineffective.

Above: The 1938 Type 62 prototype accompanies an early Type 82 Kübelwagen on test in the Black Forest. Ferdinand Porsche looks on with interest at the most recent, and ultimately highly successful, offshoot of his People's Car.

Above: Two versions of the Type 62 come to a halt while photographs are taken to record the road-test for posterity. The extra pair of wheels were designed to help the vehicle traverse rough terrain without bottoming out.

Left: By 1940, production of the final Type 82 design was in full swing. The bodies were manufactured by Ambi-Budd in Berlin, which was, ironically, an American-owned company. The completed shells were sent by rail to Wolfsburg.

In November of that year, another version was built, based this time on the much-improved VW38 sedan. The result was a far superior vehicle which clearly demonstrated that the concept was worth pursuing. This VW38 variation, the Porsche Type 62, was equipped with curvaceous open bodywork but no doors – simple canvas flaps provided weather protection when needed. Mechanically, the vehicle was unchanged from its civilian counterpart, the 985cc, flat-four, air-cooled engine providing all the power necessary for such a lightweight machine.

In 1939, a new prototype was displayed at the Vienna Fair which had the designation Type 62 (or VW62). This was the result of a collaboration between Porsche and the Trutz coachworks in Gotha, a company well versed in building military machinery. The Type 62 was a simple, slab-sided vehicle with a sharply sloping front and an abruptly cut-off back, separate fenders and a crude but well-proportioned canvas top. In tests, the Type 62 acquitted itself well, the light weight and rear-mounted engine allowing the Porsche-designed prototype to cope with slippery conditions with ease. However, the inadequate ground clearance remained a problem and prevented the vehicle from gaining acceptance in military circles – it simply could not cope with rough terrain. Porsche tried fitting 18in diameter wheels in place of the regular 16in design, but that did little to help, so it was back to the drawing board.

Kübelwagen

The result was the Type 82, a vehicle similar in style to the Type 62 but with one major improvement: far greater ground clearance. This was achieved, at the front, by relocating the stub axles further down the steering knuckle and, at the back, by the addition of a pair of reduction boxes, one at the end of each rear axle. The result was an increase in ground clearance from 220mm (8.6in) to 290mm (11.4in) at a stroke. Adding these reduction boxes solved another problem – the design brief called for a vehicle which could be driven at the walking pace of a soldier carrying a back-pack. This was judged to be 4km/h (2.5mph) but, with standard gearing, the slowest a Type 62 could be driven was 8km/h (5mph). Reduction boxes allowed the overall gearing to be lowered still further and thus another problem was solved. Even with two-wheel drive, the Type 82 became an accomplished off-road vehicle, thanks to the addition of a simple limited slip differential system. Unfortunately, this was to prove troublesome and unreliable and it took a further two years of development in the field to finally cure the problems.

Production began in earnest in 1940, with the chassis and drivetrain assembled in KdF-Stadt and the bodies by the American-owned Ambi-Budd company in Berlin. Partly due to its bucket-style seating (*Kübelsitz*) and partly due to its shape, the new vehicle soon earned itself the nickname of *Kübelwagen* or, literally,

Below: Field-Marshal Rommel, the "Desert Fox," swore he owed his life to the Kübelwagen when his driver strayed into a minefield. The vehicle's light weight prevented any mines from being detonated.

Right: In all theaters of war, the Kübelwagen proved to be popular with its drivers. Its supreme reliability and excellent off-road capabilities tended to make up for its barely adequate power output.

The Type 82 Kübelwagen remains the best-known of all wartime derivations of the KdF-Wagen. The simple, but rugged, Jeep-like vehicle saw extensive use throughout World War II. Although only supplied with two-wheel-drive, the Type 82 was a most accomplished off-road vehicle. Due to its light weight, the Kübelwagen proved to be particularly well-suited for use on both the Russian front – where thick, glutinous mud proved to be the downfall of heavier machines – and the North African desert, where it was able to cope with soft sand. Reliable and easy to maintain, the Type 82 was one of the most successful military vehicles ever.

SPECIFICATIONS

Engine: Horizontally opposed, air-cooled four cylinder. **Construction:** Two-piece cast magnesium-alloy crankcase split vertically with separate cast-iron cylinders and cast aluminum alloy pistons. Four main bearings. Cast aluminum cylinder heads with siamesed inlet ports. **Bore and stroke:** 75mm x 64mm. **Capacity:** 1131cc (69ci). **Valves:** Pushrod operated overhead. **Compression ratio:** n/a. **Fuel system:** Mechanical fuel pump; single Solex carburetor. **Maximum power:** 25bhp (31 US hp) at 3,000rpm. **Maximum torque:** 7.60mkg at 2,000rpm.

Transmission: Four-speed manual, non-synchromesh transaxle with integral final drive unit. Limited slip differential. Two-piece casing. **Gear ratios:** First – 3.60; second – 2.07; third – 1.25; fourth – 0.80; reverse – 6.60. **Final drive ratio:** 4.43:1. **Reduction gear ratio:** 1.4:1

Brakes: Cable-operated drums on all four wheels

Steering: Worm and nut

Suspension: Front: Fully independent with transverse, multi-leaf torsion bars and telescopic dampers. King- and link-pin design. Rear: Fully independent swing-axle with twin solid torsion bars and lever arm dampers. Reduction gears on rear axles.

Wheels and tires: 4J x 16in pressed steel wheels. 5.25 x 16 cross-ply tires.

Dimensions: Length: 3740mm (12ft 3.2in). Width: 1600mm (5ft 3in). Height: Top raised 1650mm (5ft 5in); Top lowered 1111mm (3ft 7.7in). Wheelbase: 2400mm (7ft 10.5in). Dry weight: 725kg (1598lb).

Peformance: Maximum speed: 80km/h (50mph). Acceleration: 0-96km/h (60mph): n/a. Fuel consumption: 8lts/100km (30mpg).

Number built: (1940-1945) 50,000

Owner: Bruce Crompton

Above: The dashboard layout was quite unlike that of any previous vehicle. In the center is the speedometer and switch gear, while to the left is a small stowage area. Either side of the speedometer is a pair of fuse boxes, while at the base of the folding windshield are two windshield wiper motors. Note the grab rail.

Above: In common with all other KdF models, the emergency (hand) brake was located between the front seats. Note the wooden duckboards on the floor ahead of the seating.

Right: The Kübelwagen was one of the most successful military vehicles used by the Wehrmacht. The simple, slab-sided body was produced by Ambi-Budd in Berlin. Note the sharply sloping nose, which allowed the driver to view the road ahead more easily, the front-mounted spare wheel and the crude weather protection.

Above: The engine for the early Kübelwagens was the original 30hp, 985cc unit but this example, having been built in 1944, uses the more powerful 1131cc engine. Engine access is very good. Note the air-filter.

Above: Most Kübelwagens were equipped with tools of some kind to help the occupants dig themselves out of an awkward situation. An ax and a shovel were typically fitted.

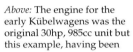

Right: When conditions allowed, the windshield could be folded flat, giving the driver a better view. This feature also allowed the vehicle to be more easily transported on a train or larger truck. The Type 82 was the epitome of function over form, with nothing fitted which did not have a purpose.

Top: The top offered minimal protection against the elements, especially the cold of the Russian Front. However, something was better than nothing. Note the air intake louvers under the rear window area and the large engine cover.
Above: Most drivers preferred to run with the top down as the improved visibility made driving easier. The engine was protected from damage by a substantial skid-plate. Two tow hooks were provided to allow easy recovery.

and a slightly increased power output of just 31hp, sufficient to silence any critics who might have complained about the Type 82 not meeting the required standards.

Shortly after the Kübelwagen went into production, work began on developing an amphibious version. The project was given the factory designation Type 128 and resulted in a tub-like vehicle based on Type 82 components but with the added advantage of four-wheel drive to cope with poor terrain. The first prototype, based on a modified Kübelwagen, was put to the test in July 1940 and served to prove that, once again, Porsche's basic design was sound. By the end of September that year, a number of hand-built prototypes had undergone extensive testing in the Max-Eyth-See, near Stuttgart, these having more rounded bodywork with a hull-like lower half.

Mechanically, the Type 128 shared the same engine and basic transmission as its forebears, but drive was taken from the front of the

Above: The conditions under which the Kübelwagen was expected to operate were, at times, truly diabolical, yet the trusty Volkswagen took it all in its stride.

Right: A pre-production Type 128 in the Max-Eyth-See near Stuttgart. At the controls is Ferry Porsche. This vehicle was the forerunner of the Type 166.

"bucket-car." The term was, however, one of affection, for the Type 82 rapidly established itself as the mainstay of the German military, proving to be a match for the seemingly more sophisticated US-designed General Purpose Vehicle, or Jeep. With its air-cooled engine, the Kübelwagen was equally at home in the biting cold of the Russian front or in the desert heat of North Africa.

A Life Saver

Field-Marshal Rommel, the "Desert Fox," was a great fan of the Kübelwagen and even claimed that it had saved his life. One day, his driver strayed into a minefield, but the light weight of the vehicle prevented it from detonating any mines, although the heavier vehicle following behind was blown up and its occupants killed. Considering the versatility of the design, it is perhaps slightly ironic that, due to bureaucratic mix up, a series of 500 Kübelwagens specially adapted for use in the desert found their way to the Russian front. They performed well under the extreme conditions, as did the 500 Russian-bound Kübels that Rommel received by default…

Strictly speaking, with its modest power output, the Type 82 fell short of German military requirements, but this fact was overlooked once it had been shown that the basic design was so effective. In 1943, however, the engine was redesigned with a larger cylinder bore (75mm, 2.9in, instead of 70mm, 2.75in), which resulted in a capacity of 1,131cc

transaxle forward to a separate differential unit mounted adjacent to the front axle beam. Two driveshafts with universal joints transmitted power to the front wheels while, at both ends of the vehicle, rubber seals prevented the ingress of water into either the interior or the engine bay. Both differential units were equipped with a limited slip system and an extra, cross-country, ratio was added to the gearbox. The Type 128 could be driven in either two- or four-wheel drive modes, the selection being made by the same lever which selected cross-country gearing.

To provide motive power when in the amphibious mode, a propeller was fitted to the rear of the Type 128, with the drive being taken from the end of the crankshaft. In normal, on-road, use the propeller was hinged up out of the way but it could be swung down into position when the vehicle entered the water. It is interesting to note that the rear wheels continued to turn in the water, helping

Above: The Type 166 Schwimmwagen proved to be one of the most versatile military vehicles of all time, equally at home on land or water. Here an early production model is shown undergoing trials in the Mittelland Canal, adjacent to the factory. In the background are some of the workers' houses.

Below: The Type 128 was essentially a stretched Schwimmwagen but did not prove to as successful due to its longer wheelbase and greater bulk. With its four-wheel drive and amphibious capabilities, it was, however, a real go-anywhere machine. Its relatively deep draft – some 80cm (31.5in) – restricted its speed in water.

When the Waffen SS approached Porsche about the possibility of fitting a KdF-Wagen engine into a motorcycle, so as to produce a compact go-anywhere machine, the discussions led to the design and development of the Type 166. This fascinating amphibious vehicle had a wheelbase some 400mm (15.75in) less than that of the Kübelwagen and enjoyed the benefits of all-wheel-drive. Powered by the same air-cooled four-cylinder engine as its stablemate, the Type 166 was fitted with a propeller driven from the end of the crankshaft to provide propulsion in water. This is regarded as one of the most versatile military vehicles ever built.

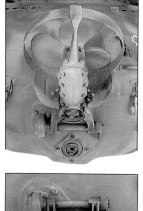

Left: When the Schwimmwagen was in water, it was commonplace to fold the windshield down. This also facilitated transportation. A cover was provided to protect the windshield when not in use. Note the single windshield wiper motor and the front-mounted spare wheel. The gas filler cap is just ahead of the windshield.

Left: The simple top folded down out of the way but offered little protection when raised. Rudimentary mudguards offered similarly minimal protection.

Left: The engine is also the later 1131cc unit but is equipped with an air-filter which draws air from above the vehicle to prevent the ingress of water. The engine is used in conjunction with a four-speed transmission which features a limited-slip differential and power take-off for the front wheels. The four-wheel-drive system was developed for the Schwimmwagen but later saw limited use on some Type 877 sedans. The drive for the propeller was taken from the end of the crankshaft. The engine bay was efficiently sealed to keep water out.

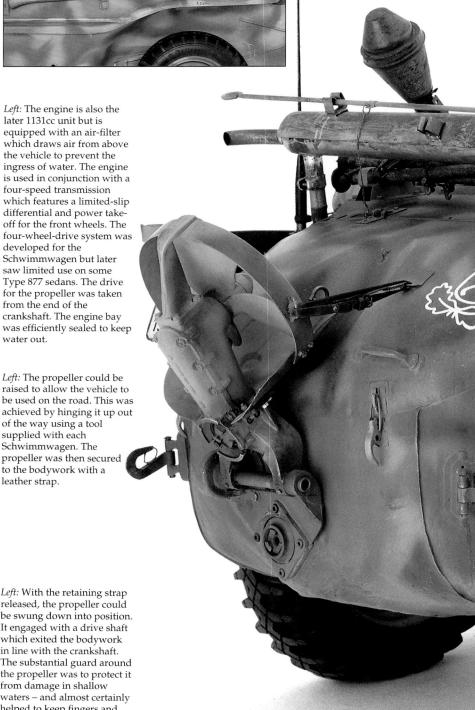

Left: The propeller could be raised to allow the vehicle to be used on the road. This was achieved by hinging it up out of the way using a tool supplied with each Schwimmwagen. The propeller was then secured to the bodywork with a leather strap.

Left: With the retaining strap released, the propeller could be swung down into position. It engaged with a drive shaft which exited the bodywork in line with the crankshaft. The substantial guard around the propeller was to protect it from damage in shallow waters – and almost certainly helped to keep fingers and toes out of harm's way!

SPECIFICATIONS

Engine: Horizontally opposed, air-cooled four cylinder. **Construction:** Two-piece cast magnesium-alloy crankcase split vertically with separate cast-iron cylinders and cast aluminum alloy pistons. Four main bearings. Cast aluminum cylinder heads with siamesed inlet ports. **Bore and stroke:** 75mm x 64mm. **Capacity:** 1131cc (69ci). **Valves:** Pushrod operated overhead. **Compression ratio:** 5.8:1. **Fuel system:** Mechanical fuel pump; single Solex carburetor. **Maximum power:** 25bhp (31 US hp) at 3,000rpm. **Maximum torque:** 7.60mkg at 2,000rpm

Transmission: Four-wheel drive with four-speed manual, non-synchromesh transaxle with integral final drive unit. Limited slip differential. Two-piece casing. **Gear ratios:** First – 3.60; second – 2.07; third – 1.25; fourth – 0.80; reverse – 6.60. **Final drive ratio:** 4.43:1. **Reduction gear ratio:** 1.4:1. Propeller driven from crankshaft.

Brakes: Cable-operated drums on all four wheels

Steering: Worm and nut

Suspension: Front: Fully independent with transverse, multi-leaf torsion bars and telescopic dampers. King- and link-pin design. **Rear:** Fully independent swing-axle with twin solid torsion bars and lever arm dampers. Reduction gears on rear axles.

Wheels and tires: 4J x 16in pressed steel wheels. 5.20 x 16 cross-ply tires.

Dimensions: Length: 3825mm (12ft 6.6in). **Width:** 1480mm (4ft 10.3in). **Height:** 1615mm (5ft 3.6in). **Wheelbase:** 2000mm (6ft 6.7in). **Dry weight:** 890kg (1962lb).

Peformance: Maximum speed: on land 80km/h (50mph); on water 10km/h (6mph). **Acceleration:** 0-96km/h (60mph): n/a. **Fuel consumption:** n/a.

Number built: (1942-1944) 14,283

Owner: Bruce Crompton

Right: The tub-like shape of the Schwimmwagen can be clearly seen in these views. The large engine access panel was designed to help prevent water from getting into the engine bay – the high sides being well above the water line.

Left: The dashboard of the Type 166 was even more rudimentary than that of the Kübelwagen. The central switch panel housed a tiny speedometer and other minor controls. In front of the driver were the instructions for selecting four-wheel-drive and use of the special low-ratio gear. A simple black three-spoke steering wheel was identical to that of the Kübel. Control levers between the seats included the gearshift lever and the selector for high and low ratios, and four-wheel-drive. The extra pedal on the floor operated an automatic greasing facility.

Left: This rear three-quarter view gives a good indication of the boat-like nature of the Schwimmwagen. Note the high-mounted exhaust system and the crude air intake grille behind the cockpit.

Left: Drive to the front wheels was achieved via these driveshafts which were located just behind the familiar king- and link-pin suspension set-up.

37

forward motion, and that the front wheels were used to steer – an indicator on the dashboard showed their position. Capable of just 10km/h (6mph) in water, the heavy (at 900kg, 1,985lb) Type 128 could still manage 80km/h (50mph) on dry land. If this amphibious machine had one failing, it was that it was too bulky, the wheelbase remaining the same as the KdF-Wagen's at 2400mm (94.5in).

Schwimmwagen

Ferry Porsche, Ferdinand's son who had worked alongside his father since 1931, recalls a visit from a Waffen SS delegation, during which he was asked if it would be possible to fit a Volkswagen engine into a motorcycle. Ferry pointed out that his father's company did not design motorcycles but asked what the problem was. It turned out that the SS was after an all-terrain vehicle which could cope with everything from hard ground to soft mud and slime. Such a vehicle needed to be lightweight and compact. The young Porsche suggested that he might be able to help and the design team returned to their office in April 1941 to come up with the Type 166. This was another amphibious vehicle developed as a result of lessons learned from the Type 128, this time with a narrower track and a wheelbase which was some 400mm (15.75in) less than that of its predecessor, making it far more maneuverable. By August, a prototype was ready for testing and it proved successful, the reduced size and 10kg (22lb) lower weight meeting the SS's brief perfectly.

The Type 166, or *Schwimmwagen* as it became known, proved to be hugely popular

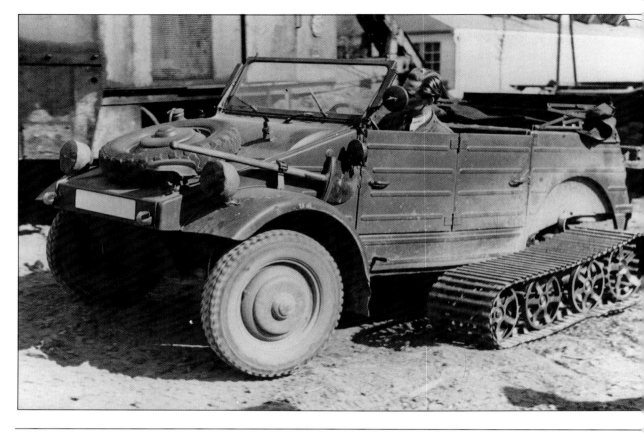

with the German Army, seeing action on all fronts. Its primary role was that of a reconnaissance vehicle, as its superb off-road capabilities allowed it to tackle terrain that no other vehicle could cope with. In most instances, it proved even more capable than a motorcycle. In total, 14,283 examples were built between 1942, when they first went into production, and 1944 when a shortage of raw materials brought things to a standstill.

Several other variations on the Type 82 theme appeared on Porsche's drawing board during the war, some of which were quite

bizarre, such as the Type 155, a half-track Kübelwagen, and the Type 157 – a model designed to run along railroad tracks. Other versions included those converted to accept twin rear wheels for better traction, radio cars, fire tenders and munitions carriers. However, two of the more practical were the Type 82E and the Type 877 (often referred to simply, but incorrectly, as the Type 87). The former was essentially a KdF-Wagen bodyshell mounted on a regular two-wheel drive Kübelwagen chassis, the greater ride height giving the vehicle better cross-country capabilities while

Left: The Type 877, known as the Kommandeurwagen, consisted of a KdF-Wagen body on the four-wheel drive Type 128 running gear, the increased ride height resulting in superior off-road capabilities. Despite the promising specification, it proved difficult to drive, especially on the road.

Right: The Type 64 (also referred to as the K-10) was one of three vehicles built to contest the planned Berlin-Rome road race of 1939. Sadly the outbreak of war prevented the event from taking place. The Type 64 clearly hinted at the possible production of a future Porsche-designed sports car.

The steering was heavy and vague, lacking any sensation of self-centering due to the four-wheel drive conversion. Even on smooth road surfaces, the Type 877 tended to weave its way down the road. It also has to be said that the sound generated by the complex transmission system was enough to drown even that generated by the noisy air-cooled engine. With a full payload, the Type 877 weighed in at a massively overweight 1,240kg (2,734lb) – more than enough for the poor 31hp engine.

But what of the basic KdF-Wagen sedan? As explained at the end of the first chapter, not one of the German workers who signed up for the Sparkarte scheme ever received their cars, although a fair proportion of them actually paid for the car in full. Was it all a giant fraud? Probably not, for the money paid into the KdF savings scheme was kept in a special account in Berlin and was found to be untouched after the war. Sadly, the money was seized by the Soviet forces and was never seen again. Up until August 1940, a total of 54 KdF sedans had been built, along with six cabriolets. All were destined for testing purposes or use by high-ranking officials. It is worthy of note that few of these officials ever appeared to use their KdF-Wagens, preferring to be seen in their more glamorous Mercedes.

Official production commenced on July 11th, 1941, somewhat late in the day to be of any use to the workers. The first cars were delivered on September 3rd and, by the time production finally ceased, on August 7th, 1944, some 630 sedans and a further 13 cabriolets had been built, again principally for use by the military or other government depart-

Left: Many versions of the Kübelwagen were built, including this slightly bizarre half-track, the Type 155. Despite the unusual means of propulsion, the Type 155 continued to rely on the conventional front wheels for steering. Other variations included dummy tanks for training, or possibly decoy, purposes. *Above:* The first production KdF-Wagens were distributed among high-ranking Nazi Party officials and other dignitaries. Seen here in 1940 are, from left to right, the cars destined for Dr. Bobo Lafferentz, Dr. Ferdinand Porsche, Gauleiter Telchow and Dr. Robert Ley, the head of the Labor Organization.

retaining the practicality of an enclosed sedan car. The Type 87 was in fact a four-wheel drive version of the regular Kübelwagen, but the designation has popularly become associated with what is more correctly known as the Type 877 – this was a KdF-Wagen sedan bodyshell on the running gear of the Type 128, four-wheel drive amphibious vehicle.

Kommandeurwagen

Known as the *Kommandeurwagen*, the Type 877 was only built in small numbers – just 667 were built between 1942 and 1944 – and, on paper at least, it clearly showed promise. However, these four-wheel drive saloons were not easy cars to drive, for the ratios in the front and rear differentials were not the same. Today, it is not uncommon to find four-wheel drive vehicles in which different amounts of torque are applied to the front and rear wheels, but that is achieved by such technology as viscous couplings and the like. With no such technical delights available at the time, the Type 877 relied upon a certain amount of slippage on loose surfaces to prevent the drivetrain from tying itself in knots.

With the prospect of a war looming large on the horizon, Porsche was forced to turn his attentions towards developing military versions of the KdF-Wagen, one such example being the Type 82E. This vehicle featured the regular sedan body mounted on the high-riding running gear of the Type 82 Kübelwagen. The resultant increase in ground clearance greatly improved its off-road capabilities, thereby rendering it suitable for use by the Wehrmacht in all theaters of war. In 1941, a four-wheel-drive version, the Type 877 or *Kommandeurwagen*, was developed from the Type 82E, although only a relatively small number of these were built.

Left: KdF-model Beetles were all fitted with this round gas tank. The bracket in front of it is for carrying the spare wheel. Note the substantial front bulkhead design and exposed front suspension.

Above: The dashboard layout is virtually identical to that of the last of the pre-war prototypes, with its two open glove boxes and a single gauge panel housing the speedometer. Note the blanking plate which now has the famous KdF "cog-wheel" logo stamped into it. The steering wheel is same as that of earlier models.

Above: The chassis plate, to the left of the gas tank, shows year of manufacture, weight and model type.

Above: The high-riding stance of the Type 82E is due to the adoption of the reduction-type rear axle and front spindle assemblies usually fitted to the Type 82 Kübelwagen.

Above: From the rear, the 1943 military Type 82E looks very little different to the earlier 1938 VW38 prototypes. Note the single exhaust tail pipe which exits centrally under the rear valance.

Above: The semaphore turn signals are mounted externally in metal boxes located at the base of each windshield pillar.

Above: From the front, it is easy to appreciate the increased ride height. The idea behind this was to give the Type 82E better off-road capabilities. Note the total lack of embellishment – after all, this was intended to be a serious military vehicle. The simple blade bumpers and bumper guards are similar to those fitted to the VW38.

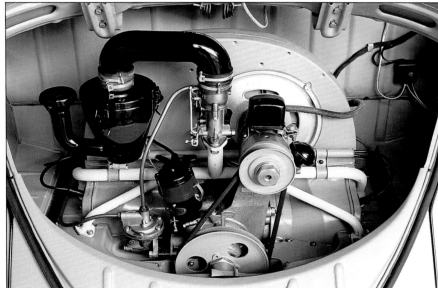

Above: The 1131cc engine was first introduced early in 1943 and produced 31hp at 3,300rpm. This was only just sufficient to meet the minimum requirements laid down by the German military authorities. Note the air-filter designed to cope with desert conditions.

Below: In the absence of a fuel gauge, a three position (on-off-reserve) fuel tap was fitted. This could be operated, at a stretch, by the driver's foot. It is shown here in the "on" position.

Left: The running boards of the Type 82E differed from the later versions by having these metal end caps fitted over the top of the rubber molding.

SPECIFICATIONS

Engine: Horizontally opposed, air-cooled four cylinder. **Construction:** Two-piece cast magnesium-alloy crankcase split vertically with separate cast-iron cylinders and cast aluminum alloy pistons. Four main bearings. Cast aluminum cylinder heads with siamesed inlet ports. **Bore and stroke:** 75mm x 64mm. **Capacity:** 1131cc (69ci). **Valves:** Pushrod operated overhead. **Compression ratio:** 5.8:1. **Fuel system:** Mechanical fuel pump; single Solex 26VFJ carburetor. **Maximum power:** 25bhp (31 US hp) at 3,300rpm. **Maximum torque:** 49lb ft at 2,000rpm.

Transmission: Four-speed manual, non-synchromesh transaxle with integral final drive unit. Two-piece casing. **Gear ratios:** First – 3.60; second – 2.07; third – 1.25; fourth – 0.80; reverse – 6.60. **Final drive ratio:** 4.43:1. Reduction gear ratio: 1.4:1

Brakes: Cable-operated drums on all four wheels

Steering: Worm and nut

Suspension: Front: Fully independent with transverse, multi-leaf torsion bars and telescopic dampers. King- and link-pin design. Rear: Fully independent swing-axle with twin solid torsion bars and lever arm dampers. Reduction gears on rear axles.

Wheels and tires: 4J x 16in pressed steel wheels. 5.20 x 16 cross-ply tires.

Dimensions: Length: 4070mm (13ft 4.2in). **Width:** 1540mm (5ft 0.6in). **Height:** 1600mm (5ft 3in). **Wheelbase:** 2400mm (7ft 10.5in). **Dry weight:** 780kg (1720lb).

Peformance: Maximum speed: 80km/h (50mph). **Acceleration:** 0-96km/h (60mph): n/a. **Fuel consumption:** n/a.

Number built: (1942-1944) 546

Owner: Hermann Walter

ments, although some remained at the factory for use by the staff.

Throughout this period, the matter of model designation has grown to become something of a nightmare as far as the historian is concerned, for it would appear that the same model might be given two different design numbers, while two others might share the same designation. It is, therefore, worth taking a look at what appears to be a contradictory puzzle. The original numbers used by Porsche related directly to the chronology of the various projects, hence Project No 1 was the first, No 12, the twelfth, etc. The first recognizable prototypes of the People's Car were the V1, V2 and V3 models, of which the latter appeared in three guises: V3-I, V3-II and V3-III. Next in line was the VW30, the series of 30 vehicles as tested by the SS, followed by the VW38 and VW39, whose numbers appear to relate more to the year of construction rather than any project number or quantity.

When the first pre-production KdF-Wagen was built, it was given the Porsche designation Type 60, with a series of "K" number suffixes used to differentiate between differing body styles. Amongst these was the K-1 sedan, K-8 sedan with sun-roof, K-9, the convertible KdF-Wagen, and the K-10, a series of three sports cars built by Porsche to contest the 1939 Berlin-Rome road race (also known as

the Type 64!). There was even a K-11 which was to be a plastic-bodied version intended to side-step future material shortages.

After Type 60 came a whole host of variations, many of which progressed no further than the drawing board. A right-hand drive model (Type 66) was even considered, as was an invalid conversion (Type 67).

Above: There was a large proportion of foreign workers at the KdF factory, many of whom were forced labor. At the end of the war, when the Allies finally over-ran the surrounding area, there was chaos as many of the workers fled for safety, while others ransacked the factory.

Below: As early as 1940, there were signs of a fuel shortage and by 1943/4 the situation had become acute. Several alternatives to regular gasoline were tried, including an ingenious wood-gas generator. Shown here is a Type 82 Kübelwagen and a Type 82E sedan equipped with this conversion.

The confusion begins when some models were allocated new numbers, such as the Type 92 (the SS version of the Type 82E) which later became known as the Type 51! As we have seen, the Type 87 was a four-wheel drive Type 82, but that designation was popularly applied to the Type 877, the four-wheel drive KdF-Wagen. After the war, the designations became even more convoluted, with the Type 82 Kübelwagen becoming known as the Type 21, the Type 60 sedan becoming the Type 11 and ultimately the Type 1.

Among the considerable number of Porsche design numbers can be seen the Type 230 (VW with gas generator), Type 330 (VW sedan with combined wood/gas fuel system), Type 331 (VW with "native" fuel system) and the Type 332 (VW with anthracite coal system). These were some of the last of the wartime designs and took heed of the fact that liquid fuels were all but unobtainable. Several of these unlikely vehicles were built, in both sedan and Kübelwagen form, the conversion equipment being extremely ungainly and adding considerably to the all-up weight. Filled with coal, for instance, the Type 332 weighed some 80kg (176lb) more than the basic Type 82.

Wolfsburg Is Born

Such designs were a barometer of the way the war was going for Germany: fuel shortages and a serious lack of raw materials, along with ever-increasing air-raids, made it clear that the end was in sight. As far as the factory was concerned, it came on April 10/11th, 1945, when advancing American troops finally appeared on the horizon. They halted some 10km (6miles) short of the factory for the simple reason that their maps did not even show the town, KdF-Stadt, to exist. The occupants of the town, and workers at the factory, were keen to make contact with the Americans, preferring to place themselves in their hands rather than those of the Soviet Army, which was also approaching them.

A delegation from the town made its way perilously through the countryside, which was thick with marauding Russian troops and the remnants of SS regiments keen on seeking revenge against anyone who stood in their way. The American troops were bemused to find themselves begged by German citizens to take them prisoner and take over their town, but then many of the workers at the factory were either people who had lived in the USA before the war or were forced laborers who feared reprisals from the SS.

At this time, the town had no name. Prior to, and throughout the war, it had been referred to as the KdF-Stadt, but the cessation of hostilities meant that the KdF movement no longer existed. A new title was called for and a meeting of the town council in May 1945, held

Above: The first major air raid on the factory occurred on April 8th, 1944, when a total of almost 2,000 bombs were dropped in a single raid, which lasted less than five minutes.

Right: Three more raids took place and damage to the factory was extensive. However, in spite of this, production continued, albeit at a reduced rate.

Below: On April 29th, 1944, an American bomber crashed onto the factory, having been struck by anti-aircraft fire. Damage was severe and several vehicles were destroyed.

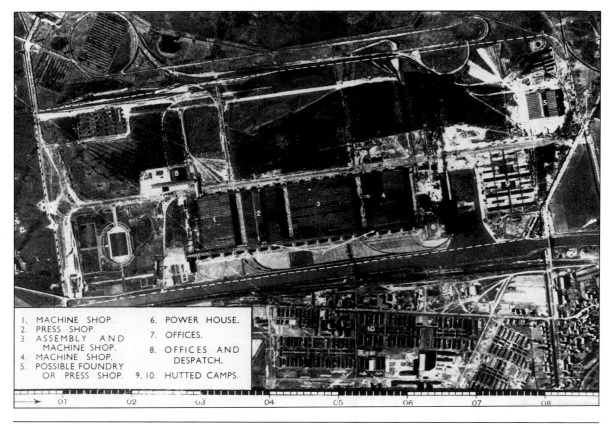

1.	MACHINE SHOP.	6.	POWER HOUSE.
2.	PRESS SHOP.	7.	OFFICES.
3.	ASSEMBLY AND MACHINE SHOP.	8.	OFFICES AND DESPATCH.
4.	MACHINE SHOP.		
5.	POSSIBLE FOUNDRY OR PRESS SHOP.	9, 10.	HUTTED CAMPS.

under the jurisdiction of the British, resulted in the Wolfsburg name being adopted, it being taken from the nearby castle, Schloss Wolfsburg. The factory was in an extremely bad way, with two thirds of the buildings having been either destroyed or severely damaged by Allied bombing raids, and many locals felt it unlikely that production would ever be able to start again.

Above: An aerial photograph of the factory taken by the US Air Force on April 19th, 1944, shows how the facility had grown in size to include a test track (at the top of the photograph) and workers' quarters (bottom). Running from left to right is the Mittelland Canal, one of the principal reasons for the site being chosen for the construction of KdF-Stadt.

Below: In 1945, members of the British Army's Royal Electrical and Mechanical Engineers took charge of the factory. Captain Bryce (REME) is seen here at his desk, behind which are pre-war technical illustrations of the KdF-Wagen. On the desk in front of him are two aluminum paperweight models of the car which were cast in the foundry.

Immediately after the war, Germany was split into sections, each coming under the control of one or other of the Allied forces. Wolfsburg, being well off the beaten track, was not initially paid much heed and found itself under British control. Only later did the Soviets realize how important the site could be and show any interest. Following almost six long years of war, there was a desperate need for a vehicle repair facility, as the Allied lorries and jeeps were by now worn beyond further use. Under MilGov (Military Government) command, Colonel Michael McEvoy was given the task of looking after vehicle repair. He had, quite by chance, driven a KdF-Wagen in 1938 while he was working with Mercedes-Benz. McEvoy, then, above all others was quick to appreciate the worth of what he found at Wolfsburg. He quickly established a working party of REME (Royal Electrical and Mechanical Engineers) personnel to take a close look at the remains of the factory to discover what could and could not be of use. In August 1945, Major Ivan Hirst, also of the REME, was placed in control of the situation and a full appraisal of the factory was made.

Amid The Ruins

Among the ruins, there were several uncompleted Kübelwagens and many spares. It was not long before some of these vehicles were built up and put to use, their performance meeting with universal approval. However, the problem as far as production of any wholly new Kübels was concerned was that the Ambi-Budd factory in Berlin, which had produced the bodies for the factory, was now in the hands of Soviet troops. The press tooling had most likely been destroyed in Allied air raids – if not, then it was unlikely that the new owners would release it for anyone else to use.

Hirst was generally impressed with the basic design of the car, and thought that it might have a future. He looked around and rescued from the ruins machinery that had been used in production, and set about finding still more which had been dispersed to various sites in the area. With this machinery, essential work was carried out to the old army vehicles which had been sent to Wolfsburg for repair. Hirst also managed to get one or two KdF sedans up and running, painting one of them khaki green and sending it off to British Army headquarters for appraisal. Much to his surprise, an order for some 20,000 vehicles came back by return. Even the Americans, French and Soviets expressed an interest in acquiring some examples.

Had the Kübelwagen tooling not been lost, the simplest solution would have been to build new versions of the Type 82, but instead Hirst had to consider assembling the Type 60

Tele GIFHORN MILITARY Ext 705
Ref:- 111/MG/65/V2

SUBJECT: Credit for Volkswagenwerk.

To:- Braunschweigische Staatsbank
From:- 111 Mil Gov Det.

1. It is confirmed that Volkswagenwerk G.H.B.H. have been ordered by Military Government to produce more than 20.000 Volkswagen vehicles. To carry out this order it is estimated a credit loan of RM 20.000.000,- will be required.

2. All the vehicles produced will be requisitioned by Military Government on A.Gp. Form 80 G which will state that 35% of the price is to be credited to the Loan Account.

3. The vehicles will be paid for by the Regierungs-Hauptkasse as detailed in Control Commission Finance Div Technical Instruction No 39.

4. All Accounts of Volkswagenwerk will operate as a/cs blocked under Mil Gov Law 52 and releases will only be made on the approval of a Mil Gov officer.

GIFHORN
17 Sep 45

R. BISSET   Major
SO II Finance
111 Det Mil Gov

(KdF sedan) instead. The press shop at Wolfsburg had been damaged quite severely, but fortunately most of the tooling was still in a usable condition and could be put back to work. Here, Hirst was able to set in motion the production of a new series of sedan models. These were based upon the chassis of the two-wheel drive Kübelwagen (Type 82) and were effectively what had been known under

Above: Major Ivan Hirst was largely responsible for overseeing operations at Wolfsburg. With him is Karl Schmücker, his secretary, and uncle of the future Chief Executive, Tony Schmücker.

Below: The 1946 production line, showing cars almost ready to leave the factory. Note they are still based on Kübelwagen running gear.

Above: A MilGov memo referring to requirements for financing the British Army order for some 20,000 Beetles, dated September 17th, 1945.

German control as the Type 82E except that they were fitted with the larger 1131cc, 31hp engine. These vehicles were later redesignated the Type 51 by Hirst, the Type 53 being a sunroof model while the Type 55 was to have been a cabriolet. The Type 82 Kübel was retitled the Type 21 but, of course, never saw production again.

It was impossible for the factory to remain under British military control for any longer than was absolutely necessary, but the matter of who should run it first needed to be resolved. Hirst set about appointing a new management structure, with its members being taken from those VW personnel who had successfully come through the de-Nazification process that was taking place in Germany, along with a few "outsiders." The whole process was a mass of confusion, according to Ivan Hirst, as he recalled that some members of the new management were considered unacceptable by his superiors and

had to be replaced, only to be reinstated following an appeal. Eventually, after what Hirst referred to as a game of musical chairs, a relatively stable management was established and the task of undertaking full-scale production was ready to be addressed. As far as production workers were concerned, most were recruited from PoWs currently being released from holding camps in the British Zone, while others were local townspeople who had worked at the factory in the past.

British Control

Holding the whole structure together was a British board which was also responsible for the town of Wolfsburg, with Major Hirst and an assistant looking after financial matters and Colonel Charles Radclyffe taking responsibility for the industrial side. Ivan Hirst, although always heralded as being the man responsible for getting the Volkswagen back on its feet, always keenly emphasized that it was a team effort, with Germans and British working alongside each other towards a common goal.

When Germany surrendered at the end of World War II, the matter of wartime reparations was raised – a system whereby other countries could claim some form of damages against Germany for the losses and costs incurred fighting the Nazis. A list of possible assets was drawn up, with Wolfsburg not unnaturally being included. One of the first to show an interest was Australia, a country that had never had a worthwhile engineering industry. However, because the factory was being used for the repair of military vehicles,

Above: Colonel Charles R. Radclyffe, CBE, DSO, was head of light mechanical engineering in the MilGov organization. He was Major Ivan Hirst's immediate superior and operated from headquarters at Minden.

Left: Demand for the Beetle steadily increased, putting greater pressure on the already overstretched production lines. Much of the work was very labor-intensive. Here, bodyshells are being welded in a jig.

the MilGov had placed a four-year reserve on Wolfsburg and Australia was not prepared to wait that long.

Another possible new owner was America with the Ford factory showing a good deal of interest in the plant. The MilGov was quite taken with the idea of Ford having control, as it was felt that there were many advantages to a car manufacturing company running the Volkswagen factory. Ford, of course, already had a plant at Cologne. Hirst attended a number of meetings, which included representatives from Ford in Great Britain, only to discover that they, too, shared many of the problems which beset the Volkswagen factory, the worst being a shortage of raw materials. Hirst so impressed the people from Ford that he was offered a job, but politely turned it down, preferring to see the Volkswagen project through to completion. Some time later, in 1948, Henry Ford II visited the Wolfsburg plant for talks with Charles

Below: A view along the factory taken from the roof of the office block in 1946. The vehicles parked below are of interest for, along with seven Beetle sedans are, to the extreme left, a unique Kübelwagen pick-up, a Beetle van (fifth from left) and, next to it, a pre-war DKW. The patches of soil next to the roadway were cultivated, at Ivan Hirst's request, in an effort to make the factory seem more cheerful, while the area to the extreme right was turned over to food production.

Above: Popularly known as the "Radclyffe Roadster," this unique two-seater was built in the experimental workshops by Rudolph Ringel. It became the regular summer transport for Colonel Radclyffe.

Below: Ivan Hirst firmly believed there was a need to expand the model range and asked Ringel to build a cabriolet. Although the result was attractive enough, the windshield regularly broke because it was insufficiently supported.

Radclyffe, but when he realized how close the site was to the Soviet Zone, he lost interest. Anti-communist feelings ran high in the USA at the time.

Another possible new keeper was the British Rootes organization under the leadership of Sir William, later Lord, Rootes. He made a trip to Wolfsburg to take a look at the machine tools which were in use there, most notably a large press used to stamp out the roof sections. However, this particular piece of equipment had been damaged beyond eco-

nomic repair in the war, so Rootes began to lose interest. Ivan Hirst showed him round the remainder of the factory and told the British industrialist of his plan to put the Volkswagen back into production. Sir William politely smiled and said to Hirst, "It's been a nice day, young man, but if you think you're going to get any cars built here, you're a fool!" Many years later, Lord Rootes confessed to Wing Commander Berryman, also of the MilGov organization, that he should perhaps have shown rather more interest…

Close Inspection

With the war against Japan still under way, arrangements were made later in 1945 for a number of engineering specialists to visit Germany to examine firsthand the latest techniques employed by German industry. According to Ivan Hirst, the principal objective of this tour was to see if anything could be learned that might be put to use in the war in the Far East. However, although Japan surrendered not long after hostilities came to an end in Europe, two Volkswagens were still transported back to the United Kingdom for further investigation at the Humber factory. There, technicians examined the cars in detail and came to the somewhat surprising decision that there was little they could learn from the Volkswagen design. Considering how crude the majority of British vehicles were at the time, this view was clearly short-sighted.

It was around this time, in 1946, that an interesting variation on the Beetle was built at the factory. Colonel Michael McEvoy, his interest in motorsport not having been dulled by almost six long years of war, came to Hirst one day and suggested they build a Volkswagen-based racing car. Hirst was less than impressed with the idea, rightly believing that the factory had more than enough on its plate without getting side-tracked with such a whimsical project. However, McEvoy's enthusiasm did set Hirst thinking, so he sketched out an idea for a two-seat Volkswagen roadster and asked Rudolph Ringel, head of the experimental shop, to build a prototype. This car was offered by Hirst to Colonel Charles Radclyffe, his chief at headquarters, for use during the summer months. Subsequently known by enthusiasts

the world over as "the Radclyffe Roadster," the attractive two-seater saw regular use before eventually disappearing, probably scrapped by Volkswagen personnel. The same fate almost certainly befell a crude cabriolet Beetle which Hirst had Ringel build for his personal use.

At this time, two well-established coach-building companies approached Volkswagen with regard to producing convertible Beetles. One of these was Wilhelm Karmann GmbH, the other Joseph Hebmüller and Sons. Karmann, of Osnabrück, had a long history of building high-quality cabriolets based on a variety of chassis from companies such as

Hansa-Lloyd and Adler. After the war, Karmann visited Wolfsburg with a view to buying a Volkswagen chassis on which to build a convertible Beetle. However, due to the restrictions placed on German citizens which prevented them from buying a car at this time, Karmann was unsuccessful in his approach. However, his persistence paid off and, in November 1946, he was given the 10,000th car to be built since the war.

Further chassis were soon made available and two prototypes were built at the Karmann works. The first of these was a crude conversion with external hinges on the top mechanism and no rear windshield. The

Above: Despite shortages of raw materials, production at Wolfsburg gradually continued to increase until, in October 1946, the 10,000th car left the factory. This was a justifiable cause for celebration for, less than a year earlier, the future had looked very bleak.

Left: Karmann built two cabriolet prototypes which, once the problem of chassis flex had been ironed out, met with factory approval. However, a shortage of raw materials meant the project had to be put on hold.

Right: Dutchman Ben Pon (third from left) ordered a batch of six cars late in 1947. However, when he arrived at the factory, only five were ready. This was to be Volkswagen's first ever export sale.

second was much improved, with wind-down rear side windows, a glass rear windshield and a more sophisticated top frame. However, excessive chassis flex was a major problem, necessitating the addition of a substantial reinforcing member under each sill. Despite the success of the Karmann prototypes, all talk of series production was fruitless due to a lack of the essential raw materials, such as sheet steel and fabric for the folding roof. Not for a further two years was Karmann able to resume work in earnest.

Expanding Horizons

Hebmüller's story was similar to that of Karmann, with official permission being granted to build a series of prototypes which, with Volkswagen's approval, would make way for a production run. Once the problems of a lack of rigidity had been overcome, Hebmüller was able to satisfy Volkswagen that his roadster was ready for production. However, there were political moves afoot in Germany which would have a profound effect on the future of the company.

Hirst and Radclyffe were confident that the Beetle had a future and, in 1947, visited the Paris Motor Show to take a look at the opposition, so to speak. Few cars impressed them other than the Skoda, which was also a rear-engined, small car, although water- rather than air-cooled. On their return to Wolfsburg, the matter of who would take over the running of the factory was raised again. Times were changing in Europe, with the Soviet Union, formerly an ally, becoming more and more isolationist in its outlook. It would possibly soon not be wise for the British to have a presence so close to the Soviet sector.

Above: Joseph Hebmüller also approached the factory about building a convertible version of the Beetle. His design was for a very stylish two-seater, not at all unlike the original "Radclyffe Roadster." The first Hebmüller prototypes were completed in 1948, having been based on very early post-war cars. Shown here is an early production model parked outside the Hebmüller family home at Wulfrath in Germany.

In the meantime, Ben Pon arrived at Wolfsburg wishing to order some cars. He was the strong-willed Dutchman to whom Ferdinand Porsche had agreed to make available the first export models once the war was over. Considering the vehement anti-German feelings held by the majority of the Dutch, Pon was clearly either foolish or a man convinced of the Beetle's worth. How else could someone expect to sell a German product in post-war Holland? However, history was to prove that Pon was certainly no fool. His order for six cars was duly accepted but when he returned to the factory to collect them, only five were ready, the sixth having fallen foul of the some-

what unreliable production line. This episode marked the fulfilment of the first export order for a Volkswagen.

Hirst began the search for a person qualified to head the factory and started to interview suitable people. He came to hear of one Heinz Nordhoff, formerly of Opel. There, he had been responsible for overseeing Opel truck production and, as a result, had been awarded an honorary title of Economic Leader during the war. This title prevented him from holding any executive position at a German facility in the US sector – the Americans considered him possibly to have too many Nazi connections, although this proved not to be the case. As the

When the British Army appointed Heinz Nordhoff the General Director of Volkswagen in January 1948, the factory was producing some 2,500 cars per month. The vehicles, however, were little more than upgraded versions of the old pre-war prototypes, equipped with the 1131cc engine of the Schwimmwagen. Volkswagens of this era, as typified by the example shown here, were basic in the extreme, without chrome trim or any other non-functional adornment. However, Nordhoff realized that, for the Volkswagen sedan to appeal to a wider market, changes would have to be made and the following year, a special export model was introduced.

SPECIFICATIONS

Engine: Horizontally opposed, air-cooled four cylinder. **Construction:** Two-piece cast magnesium-alloy crankcase split vertically with separate cast-iron cylinders and cast aluminum alloy pistons. Four main bearings. Cast aluminum cylinder heads with siamesed inlet ports. **Bore and stroke:** 75mm x 64mm. **Capacity:** 1131cc (69ci). **Valves:** Pushrod operated overhead. **Compression ratio:** 5.8:1. **Fuel system:** Mechanical fuel pump; single Solex 26VFI carburetor. **Maximum power:** 25bhp (31 US hp) at 3,300rpm. **Maximum torque:** 49lb ft at 2,000rpm.

Transmission: Four-speed manual, non-synchromesh transaxle with integral final drive unit. Two-piece casing. **Gear ratios:** First – 3.60; second – 2.07; third – 1.25; fourth – 0.80; reverse – 6.60. **Final drive ratio:** 4.43:1.

Brakes: Cable-operated drums on all four wheels

Steering: Worm and nut

Suspension: Front: Fully independent with transverse, multi-leaf torsion bars and telescopic dampers. King- and link-pin design. **Rear:** Fully independent swing-axle with twin solid torsion bars and lever arm dampers.

Wheels and tires: 4J x 16in pressed steel wheels. 5.20 x 16 cross-ply tires.

Dimensions: Length: 4070mm (13ft 4.2in). **Width:** 1540mm (5ft 0.6in). **Height:** 1500mm (4ft 11in). **Wheelbase:** 2400mm (7ft 10.5in). **Dry weight:** 780kg (1720lb).

Peformance: Maximum speed: 97km/h (60mph). **Acceleration:** 0-96km/h (60mph): c27sec. **Fuel consumption:** n/a

Number built: (1948) 19,244

Owner: Hermann Walter

Below: The shape of the interior light had now been finalized as a round design.

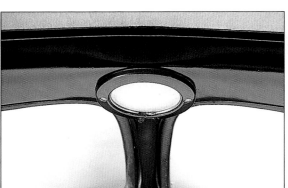

Above: The dashboard layout differed little from that of the VW38 prototypes. The right-hand blanking panel featured the familiar VW logo. All visual references to the old KdF movement had now disappeared. The speedometer design changed little.

Left: The semaphore turn signals were now located in the door pillars where they would remain until their demise in the late 1950s.

Right: With the exception of the bumpers and licence plate light, the profile of the Beetle would remain unchanged until a large rear window and windshield were introduced in August 1957.

Left: The so-called "Pope's Nose" licence plate light also incorporated the brake warning light. On early vehicles, the licence plate was mounted on a raised pressing in the deck lid.

Right: The original Renault 4CV shared several design features with the Beetle. Many people believe that Porsche's ideas were copied by the French company.

increased at a rate that surprised even Hirst. When German currency reform took place, in June 1948, the economy expanded at a great rate. Suddenly the German people became more wealthy and the prospect of owning their own cars became more achievable. By the end of the year, Wolfsburg was removed from the reparations list and allowed to breathe a little more easily. The British began to withdraw from the factory, allowing the German management to take greater responsibility. Hirst himself was demobilized during the winter of 1947/48 but remained at Wolfsburg, in a largely civilian role, to work alongside Nordhoff for what he describes as a fairly uncomfortable year and a half. He plainly felt that, if Nordhoff was to succeed, he should be allowed to run things for himself, in his own way. The MilGov board agreed and Hirst left Wolfsburg in the control of the man from Opel. Late in 1949, Charles Radclyffe finally handed the factory over to the German Minister of Economics, bringing to a close a remarkable period in the company's history.

One of the first decisions made by Nordhoff was to give the go-ahead to Karmann and Hebmüller to commence production of their cabriolets, which they manufactured from vehicles delivered to them by VW. The two companies eventually began work in earnest, Hebmüller's first production model leaving the works in Wulfrath in June 1949, and Karmann's in Osnabrück in September. Everything looked fine for the two companies

until, just one month into production, Hebmüller's workshops caught fire and were all but destroyed. Quite how the fire started remains a mystery but, following a great effort, work resumed just four weeks later. Unfortunately, Hebmüller never really recovered from this disaster and the company went into decline in 1950, eventually ceasing operations in 1951. Production of the Hebmüller roadster was transferred to the Karmann works at Osnabrück, where a further 14 examples were built, bringing the total to just 696.

Karmann fared better throughout this period, with cabriolet production growing steadily until the model became a profitable sideline to the sedan. Indeed, as time would

Above: The Volkswagen engine had remained essentially unchanged since 1943. Note the layout of the engine, with the gear-driven camshaft located below the crankshaft. Pushrods operate the overhead valves.

eventually prove, the cabriolet was destined to become the last remaining Beetle to be built in Germany.

But what of Ferdinand Porsche all this time? Sadly the far-sighted Doctor was never to play a part in seeing his beloved People's Car reach production, for he was imprisoned by the French, having been accused of employing forced labor by Pierre Peugeot, head of the French car company of the same name. The real motive behind Peugeot's incriminating outburst was probably the fact that Porsche had been invited to France by Marcel Paul, the French Minister for Industrial Production, with a view to designing a "French Volkswagen," a vehicle which would almost certainly have had a dramatic effect on the finances of existing French companies. Porsche's designs did eventually surface, somewhat modified, in the form of the Renault 4CV.

Porsche was held in prison, often in very poor conditions considering his age, until 1947. He was finally released when witnesses came forward to prove that, far from employing forced French labor, Porsche had in fact done what he could to prevent French citizens from being forcibly moved to Germany to work in his factory. His period of imprisonment did little to help the ageing Doctor who, by this time, was over 70 years old. He suffered prolonged ill-health and died on January 30th, 1951, never to witness the amazing success story of his dream car.

The new decade began with Volkswagen at last looking like it had a future. For almost five years since the end of World War II, the factory had endured hardships beyond comprehension, ranging from shortages of raw materials, labor and power, to political pushing and shoving as various governments expressed their interest – or lack of it – in the company. Only when the British finally took a firm hold of Volkswagen and then appointed Heinz Nordhoff as General Director, did the future begin to look more rosy.

By January 1950, some 86,182 Beetles had been built, although that name had not yet found its way into popular parlance. In fact, nobody can really be sure where that name came from: Ferdinand Porsche is credited with having referred to his car before the war as having the shape of a May beetle, while the American press is said to have called the car a "beetle" in the late 1940s. In Britain, the original importer, John Colborne-Baber, drove a VW and the pair were often referred to as "Colborne-Baber and his funny little beetle." All that's important is that the name stuck.

Above: On January 1st, 1948, Heinz Nordhoff took charge of the Volkswagen factory.

Below: The 10,000th car had rolled off the line in 1946. However, the workers were more concerned about a lack of food and cigarettes…

The first major milestone had been achieved in 1946 when, on October 14th, the 10,000th Beetle rolled off the assembly line. However, only a further 20 cars were to be built that year. Production sky-rocketed, in relative terms, in 1950 under Nordhoff's leadership when a total of 81,979 Beetles were assembled, almost double the production figure for the previous year. Many thought that Nordhoff had been crazy to increase production but he was right to take the decision for, at one point, there had been a waiting list of some 15,000 customers in Germany alone, along with a further 7,000 in other countries. Only by doubling production could Nordhoff guarantee being able to satisfy the demand and he was well aware that, although Volkswagen may have had a head start over most other German car manufacturers, it was only a matter of time before his competitors would re-establish themselves and be able to compete on equal terms with his company.

The problem for Nordhoff was that the company did not have the money to be able to expand in the way he wished. While the currency reform of 1948 (which replaced the Reichsmark with a new Deutschmark) gave the man in the street a new-found wealth because the currency was stabilized, it effectively reduced Volkswagen's bank balance to zero as, up until then, all financial dealings had been based on the old Reichsmark, which was worthless on the world market. Realizing that he was caught in the classic Catch 22 situation (no money meant no cars – no cars meant no money), Nordhoff contacted each of his dealers in Germany and asked them to bring to the factory as many of the new Deutschmarks as they could muster. It is a measure of the respect in which Nordhoff was held that the dealers responded by arriving at Wolfsburg with suitcases filled with money. It seems that most, if not all, realized that if they were to have a future they would have to be prepared to invest in the product.

Right: Nordhoff was most anxious to see the Beetle become a world-class car and took a keen interest in all aspects of its production. He is seen here visiting the production line sometime in the mid-1950s.

Below: Ben Pon, left, supervises the unloading of the first Beetle to go to America, aboard the *Westerdam.* Unfortunately, while the Beetle might have been ready for America, America was not ready for the Beetle.

The New World

Nordhoff was undoubtedly a man of vision, for he seemed able to see far into the future at a time when most people were still talking about the past. He knew that to survive Volkswagen needed to expand its horizons far beyond the borders of Germany and Europe – America was the key to the company's long-term success, he felt. He also appreciated, as did Ivan Hirst before him, that it would be important to ensure there was an adequate supply of spare parts so that cars could be satisfactorily serviced.

The first car which Nordhoff attempted to sell into the USA arrived there on January 17th, 1949, and marked the beginning of the American love affair with the VW. The Beetle arrived on board the *Westerdam*, accompanied by Ben Pon, the enthusiastic Dutchman who had succeeded in persuading his fellow countrymen to buy Volkswagens, even when anti-German feeling in his homeland was at its height. Pon had been sent as an envoy to the USA by Nordhoff and his brief was to assess the potential for selling the humble Volkswagen to a car-crazy America.

To set the ball rolling, an American colleague of Pon's arranged to hold a press conference on board the merchant vessel carrying that first "American" Volkswagen. Unfortunately for Pon and Nordhoff, the car received a lot of bad publicity. Despite constantly referring to the VW as the "Victory Wagen" in an effort to hide its origins, Pon was unable to persuade the Americans that the Beetle was anything other than Hitler's People's Car.

Once the car was off-loaded, Pon felt he would be able to overcome the skepticism, but he remained unable to convince the American public of its potential. He approached several automobile showrooms in an effort to enlist them as official Volkswagen agents, but again met with a lack of interest. He soon ran low on funds and was eventually forced to sell the Volkswagen, and some spares he had brought with him, for $800 to a Swedish dealer by the name of Vaughn in order to pay his hotel bill and return fare.

Pon wrote to Nordhoff, saying, "It is too early to try to sell Volkswagens in the United States. Dealers selling European cars there don't know how to service them." It seems that other importers had messed up the market for Volkswagen by convincing the public that all imports were unreliable and expensive

to maintain. The news saddened Nordhoff, for Volkswagen desperately needed some dollars with which to buy machinery and tooling from the USA. At the time, few countries were interested in receiving payment in the form of Deutschmarks. Nordhoff made the decision to visit the United States himself to see if he could solve the problem but he, too, met with the same reluctance that Pon had encountered. Nobody, it seems, believed the Volkswagen Beetle had a future, especially in the USA. The American motoring press was very critical of the product, feeling that it had nothing to offer that could not be provided by Detroit on a grander scale.

A little over a year after Ben Pon's unsuccessful visit, Nordhoff made a fresh attempt to

During the 1950s, generally most vehicles were still very plain in their appearance and the Volkswagen sedan, even in its export guise, was no exception. Because of this, there developed a whole industry dedicated to producing all kinds of accessories designed to appeal to owners who wished to personalize their cars. The accessories seen on this 1951 Export model are typical of the era. Many were functional, such as the roof rack to allow more luggage to be carried, and the mudflaps to protect the bodywork. Others, such as the exhaust trim, were intended solely to add a little glamor to what was otherwise still a very modestly-equipped family car.

SPECIFICATIONS

Engine: Oettinger-converted horizontally opposed, air-cooled four-cylinder. **Construction:** Two-piece cast Elektron alloy crankcase split vertically with separate cast-iron cylinders and cast aluminum alloy pistons. Four main bearings. Cast aluminum Okrasa cylinder heads with separate inlet ports. **Bore and stroke:** 75mm x 69.5mm. **Capacity:** 1295cc (79ci). **Valves:** Pushrod operated overhead. **Compression ratio:** 6.5:1. **Fuel system:** Mechanical fuel pump; dual Solex 32PBI carburetors. **Maximum power:** 48bhp (56 US hp) at 4,200rpm. **Maximum torque:** 66lb ft at 2,100rpm.

Transmission: Four-speed manual, non-synchromesh transaxle with integral final drive unit. Two-piece casing. **Gear ratios:** First – 3.60; second – 2.07; third – 1.25; fourth – 0.80; reverse – 6.60. **Final drive ratio:** 4.43:1.

Brakes: Hydraulically-operated drums on all four wheels

Steering: Worm and nut

Suspension: Front: Fully independent with transverse, multi-leaf torsion bars and telescopic dampers. King- and link-pin design. **Rear:** Fully independent swing-axle with twin solid torsion bars and telescopic dampers.

Wheels and tires: 4J x 16in pressed steel wheels. 5.20 x 16 cross-ply tires.

Dimensions: Length: 4070mm (13ft 4.2in). **Width:** 1540mm (5ft 0.6in). **Height:** 1500mm (4ft 11in). **Wheelbase:** 2400mm (7ft 10.5in). **Dry weight:** 780kg (1720lb).

Peformance: Maximum speed: 120km/h (75mph). **Acceleration:** 0-96km/h (60mph): 18.5sec. **Fuel consumption:** 8lts/100km (30mpg)

Number built: (1951) 93,709

Owner: Keith Seume

Left: This 1951 model has been fitted with many period accessories, a popular pastime in the days when cars were still very modestly equipped. Note the Bosch reversing light and the genuine VW accessory mudflaps. By the very early 1950s, the Beetle had grown to be more stylish, with chrome-plated bumpers adding a little glamor to the otherwise basic sedan.

Below left: Period Bosch spot and fog lamps help to make night driving a little more pleasurable. VWs were never renowned for the efficiency of their headlights.

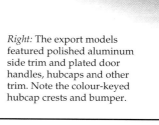

Right: The export models featured polished aluminum side trim and plated door handles, hubcaps and other trim. Note the colour-keyed hubcap crests and bumper.

Left: The semaphore turn signals have a grooved cover which was color-keyed to the main bodywork. Semaphores are the same on each side of the vehicle.

Right: Note the Becker Monza radio with clock, accessory VDM steering wheel and the bakelite covers to the glove boxes. The Bambus parcel shelf is a practical addition.

Right: The spare wheel was carried behind the front valance, ahead of the gas tank. This vehicle has been fitted with a Hazet spare wheel tool kit which clipped into the wheel center and contained most tools necessary to carry out roadside repairs. Note the accessory "eyebrows" fitted to the headlamps. These were popular additions and were intended to improve the efficiency of the lights

Below: Marketed by Oettinger in Germany, the Okrasa engine conversion boosted output to 56hp, allowing the Beetle to reach 120km/h (75mph). The kit included dual carburetors and special cylinder heads.

Above: These vents in the front quarter-panels were unique to Beetles built between January 1951 and October 1952.

Throughout the 1950s, many coachbuilding companies tried their hand at building special bodies to suit the Beetle chassis and running gear. Among the best-known of these are Hebmüller, whose two-seat roadster gained official blessing from the VW factory, and Rometsch, whose stylish coupés proved very popular. There were also many one-off creations and this, the unique Stoll Coupé, was built for a wealthy customer who, in 1952, decided that he wanted a Beetle which would stand out from the crowd. The Stoll conversion consisted of modifying the conventional sedan body into a four-seat coupé with a distinctive "humped-back" profile.

SPECIFICATIONS

Engine: Horizontally opposed, air-cooled four cylinder. **Construction:** Two-piece cast magnesium-alloy crankcase split vertically with separate cast-iron cylinders and cast aluminum alloy pistons. Four main bearings. Cast aluminum cylinder heads with siamesed inlet ports. **Bore and stroke:** 75mm x 64mm. **Capacity:** 1131cc (69ci). **Valves:** Pushrod operated overhead. **Compression ratio:** 5.8:1. **Fuel system:** Mechanical fuel pump; single Solex 26VFI carburetor. **Maximum power:** 25bhp (31 US hp) at 3,300rpm. **Maximum torque:** 49lb ft at 2,000rpm.

Transmission: Four-speed manual, non-synchromesh transaxle with integral final drive unit. Two-piece casing. **Gear ratios:** First – 3.60; second – 2.07; third – 1.25; fourth – 0.80; reverse – 6.60. Final drive ratio: 4.43:1.

Brakes: Cable-operated drums on all four wheels

Steering: Worm and nut

Suspension: Front: Fully independent with transverse, multi-leaf torsion bars and telescopic dampers. King- and link-pin design. **Rear:** Fully independent swing-axle with twin solid torsion bars and lever arm dampers.

Wheels and tires: 4J x 16in pressed steel wheels. 5.20 x 16 cross-ply tires.

Dimensions: Length: 4070mm (13ft 4.2in). **Width:** 1540mm (5ft 0.6in). **Height:** 1500mm (4ft 11in). **Wheelbase:** 2400mm (7ft 10.5in). **Dry weight:** 780kg (1720lb).

Peformance: Maximum speed: 97km/h (60mph). **Acceleration:** 0-96km/h (60mph): c27sec. **Fuel consumption:** n/a

Number built: (1952) 1

Owner: Volkswagen AG

Left: First seen in 1951, the infamous "crotch-coolers" were intended to provide ventilation but, instead, created an uncomfortable draft inside the car. The feature only lasted just under two years.

Left: The small, round horn grilles were first used in 1950. The design was superseded in 1953 by an oval-shaped grille. The horn was now located behind the left-hand grille (until 1950 it had been exposed), the other grille being a dummy. Note accessory headlamp cowls.

Left: The seats have been retrimmed in leather – this was not a factory option but specified by the original owner when the coupé conversion was executed. Note one-piece door glass.

Above: The interior of the Stoll is equipped with many period accessories: Petri steering wheel; glove box covers; 100,000km badge; St. Christopher medallion etc. Note the small round heater outlet located close to the floor – the aluminum trim can be clearly seen.

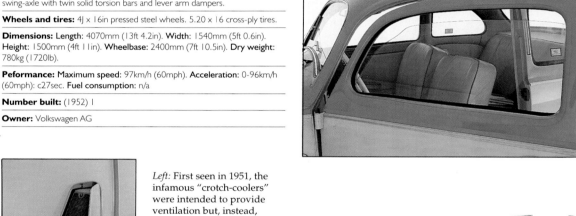

Right: The Stoll coupé is unique, but typical of the lengths people would go to make their Volkswagen stand out from the crowd. In the 1950s, many coachbuilders produced special-bodied Beetles in one form or another.

Below: The Wolfsburg crest first appeared in 1951. However, the Stoll has been fitted with a rare Australian version of the factory coat of arms. Note the cast-aluminum hood handle.

Below: Only in profile is it possible to appreciate fully the lines of the Stoll coupé. Its somewhat hump-backed appearance is debatably less pleasing than that of the regular Beetle but it still retains an elegance all of its own. The conversion did little to improve the space available to the rear seat passengers! Although the factory never offered two-tone paint (except on the cabriolet models), the combination of tan and ivory is particularly attractive in this instance.

Above: To improve the ventilation, the leading edge of the door windows were notched – this allowed the window to be wound down slightly for ventilation without causing discomfort to the passengers.

Below: The engine is the basic 1131cc, 31hp unit which was the mainstay of the Volkswagen range until 1954. In order to fit the engine under the coupé bodywork, the air-filter has been relocated to the left of the engine – the same modification was necessary on the Hebmüller models. Note the lack of sound-proofing on the bulkhead and the position of the fusebox for the rear lights.

win over the American market by appointing an exclusive US agent, a foreign car distributor by the name of Maximilian Hoffman from Chicago. Made responsible for all territories to the east of the Mississippi, Hoffman succeeded in selling no fewer than 330 Volkswagens in 1950 but, while at first sight that may have seemed impressive, the American public bought a total of over 6.6 million other cars in that year…

Early US Sales

Hoffman was a born salesman and adopted aggressive sales tactics. If he was approached by trade customers who wished to buy his more exotic Jaguars and other sports cars from him, Hoffman would occasionally suggest they stood a better chance of getting a favorable deal if they bought a Volkswagen or two. His strong-arm tactics worked well and many dealers soon discovered they could sell the Volkswagen more easily than their range of

sports cars. On one occasion, a dealer arrived at Hoffman's and was asked if he had come to collect his usual quota of sports cars but instead replied that no, he had come to collect a few more VWs – they were proving to be rather good sellers.

Those early American sales were erratic and, even though there was an increasing number of dealers handling Volkswagen's affairs in North America, Nordhoff was acutely aware there had been no effective sales strategy. What he wanted was a properly co-ordinated sales team working throughout the continent. However, Max Hoffman had always been a foreign car importer first and foremost and selling Volkswagens was only a small, albeit profitable, part of his business. He was not really too interested in the customer, but concerned himself more with selling vehicles to other dealers who could then be responsible for servicing and supplying spare parts.

This situation was in conflict with Nordhoff's (and Hirst's) ideals, whereby cars should only be sold where there was an adequate after-sales operation to look after them. He realized it would be necessary for Volkswagen to establish a full network of dealers across the country, with a full service operation to keep the cars on the road. There was no point in trying to persuade someone to buy a strange foreign car if he could not get it fixed when it went wrong, Nordhoff kept telling his people. What was happening in the USA was, therefore, in conflict with his belief that you must have a sales team backed up by an efficient service network, as was the case throughout Europe and the rest of the world. There, people were buying Volkswagen products, not only because they felt they were good vehicles, but also because they had confidence in the service and spares program.

The agreement which existed between Max Hoffman and Volkswagen finally came to an

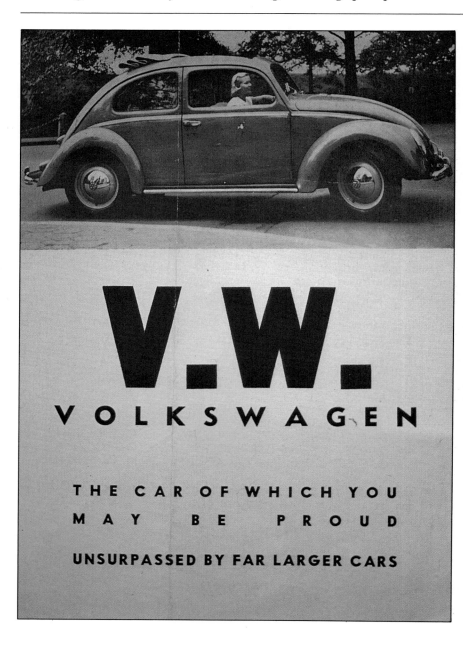

Above: Max Hoffman was the man responsible for getting sales off the ground in the USA. His sales brochures may have been modest in their presentation, but they certainly helped to get the message across.

Above: In the mid-1950s, the American sales operation was divided in two, with Geoffrey Lange taking care of the sector to the west of the Mississippi. This brochure, published in 1955, was produced by his team.

The Amazing Volkswagen

Fun to drive.

Easy to park.

Low initial cost.

Low fuel consumption.

Extremely low maintenance cost.

Upkeep averages less than bus fare.

Plenty of leg room.

Air-cooled—no winter troubles.

For

Economical — Smooth — Effortless

Driving — Take a ride in

The Amazing Volkswagen

Almost trouble-free transportation.

Hugs the road
like a carpet !

end in 1953. This left America wide open as far as VW sales were concerned, so Nordhoff, painfully aware of the fact that neither he nor his managers at Wolfsburg had any idea of how to tackle the market, studied a map of the North America and divided the country into two halves – one to the east and the other to the west of the Mississippi river. On the western side, where the Beetle had already gained considerable respect, VW's sales representative was Geoffrey Lange. Lange found to Nordhoff's pleasure that a lot of good work had been done by a customer of Max Hoffman, John von Neumann of California, who had appreciated the finer points of the Porsche-designed Volkswagen from the very beginning. Lange, much to Nordhoff's relief, was soon able to bring some order to the confusion which had reigned in the USA.

A Sixth Sense

To cover the areas to the east of the Mississippi dividing line, Nordhoff sent Will Van de Kamp across to the USA. He had previously worked as a field represesentative for Volkswagen in Germany and was someone with unshakable confidence in the products Wolfsburg had to offer. He was soon able to persuade potential dealers of the benefits of becoming part of the Volkswagen sales network. Van de Kamp arrived in the USA in January 1954 and from the word go appeared to have the powers of a clairvoyant when it came to choosing new Volkswagen dealers. While others might have taken the more obvious route of appointing established automotive retailers, Van de Kamp often chose to give someone an agency because he had a type of "sixth sense" about that person's

Above: The eastern sector was placed in the care of Will Van de Kamp, who had previously worked as a field representative in Germany. This was the brochure intended for the eastern half of the USA.

Right: With the American economy continuing to expand, air travel became very fashionable. In retrospect, it is a little surprising that the humble Beetle should have met with such success – it was, after all, a car designed for people with little money to spend.

For the 1953 model year, Volkswagen finally decided to increase the size of the rear window from its former "split" design to the far larger "oval." This brought about an increase in glass area of some 23 percent. There were few other major changes although it is worth noting that the dashboard had been substantially redesigned the previous year, the former two-pod symmetrical dashboard layout having been dropped in favor of a new asymmetrical design which placed the speedometer in front of the driver. Bigger changes were afoot at the end of the year when a new 1192cc, 36hp engine was introduced, the first engine redesign in almost ten years.

SPECIFICATIONS

Engine: Horizontally opposed, air-cooled four cylinder. **Construction:** Two-piece cast magnesium-alloy crankcase split vertically with separate cast-iron cylinders and cast aluminum alloy pistons. Four main bearings. Cast aluminum cylinder heads with siamesed inlet ports. **Bore and stroke:** 75mm x 64mm. **Capacity:** 1131cc (69ci). **Valves:** Pushrod operated overhead. **Compression ratio:** 5.8:1. **Fuel system:** Mechanical fuel pump; single Solex 26VFI carburetor. **Maximum power:** 25bhp (31 US hp) at 3,300rpm. **Maximum torque:** 49lb ft at 2,000rpm.

Transmission: Four-speed manual, non-synchromesh transaxle with integral final drive unit. Two-piece casing. **Gear ratios:** First – 3.60; second – 2.07; third – 1.25; fourth – 0.80; reverse – 6.60. **Final drive ratio:** 4.43:1.

Brakes: Cable-operated drums on all four wheels

Steering: Worm and nut

Suspension: Front: Fully independent with transverse, multi-leaf torsion bars and telescopic dampers. King- and link-pin design. Rear: Fully independent swing-axle with twin solid torsion bars and telescopic dampers.

Wheels and tires: 4J x 15in pressed steel wheels. 5.20 x 15 cross-ply tires.

Dimensions: Length: 4070mm (13ft 4.2in). Width: 1540mm (5ft 0.6in). Height: 1500mm (4ft 11in). Wheelbase: 2400mm (7ft 10.5in). Dry weight: 780kg (1720lb).

Peformance: Maximum speed: 97km/h (60mph). Acceleration: 0-96km/h (60mph): c27sec. Fuel consumption: n/a

Number built: (1953) 151,323

Owner: John Maxwell

Below: This was the last year that the 1131cc engine was used in the export models, although it did continue for a while in certain standard examples. By now the engine had been in production for ten years, first having seen service in the wartime Kübelwagen and Schwimmwagen. Although it could never have been accused of being a powerful engine, it was supremely reliable.

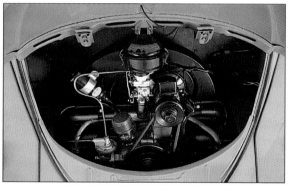

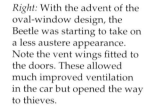

Above: The big change this year was the new oval-shaped rear window, the glass area being increased by some 23 percent. Note the trim molding round the window rubber. This feature first appeared on the last of the split-window models in 1952.

Right: With the advent of the oval-window design, the Beetle was starting to take on a less austere appearance. Note the vent wings fitted to the doors. These allowed much improved ventilation in the car but opened the way to thieves.

Left: Only minor changes were made under the front hood: the stay to hold the lid open was shortened slightly and the size of the gas filler changed from 40mm (1.57in) to 80mm (3.15in) in diameter. Note the almost ubiquitous Hazet spare-wheel toolkit, a popular, and practical, accessory of the time.

Left: In October 1952, the rear light units were redesigned to incorporate stop-light lenses in the top of the housings. This was a considerable improvement over the previous, tiny single brake light fitted on earlier models.

Right: The hood handle was redesigned, now being a chrome-plated casting as opposed to polished aluminum.

Above: This design of dashboard first appeared in 1952 with the last of the split-window models. However, note the steering wheel is still the old style, with spokes that partially obscure the driver's view of the basic instrumentation.

Above: The bumpers were now of a plain design, lacking the ribbing of the earlier style. The badge bar is an accessory part, as are the two Hella horns. Note the way in which the windshield wipers park, favoring a right-hand drive vehicle.

abilities. With Geoffrey Lange in the west and Van de Kamp in the east, Nordhoff was pleased to be able to establish a network of dealers across America which was still recognizable almost a quarter of a century later.

Quite why the American public suddenly appeared to take a shine to the Volkswagen cannot be entirely explained by Lange's or Van de Kamp's enthusiasm. After all, no matter how good the salesman is, you still have to tempt the customer into the showroom. It is possible that, by the early 1950s, the American public was becoming used to the thought of buying imported products of all types. Motoring enthusiasts in the USA had long appreciated that if you wanted a fine-handling sports car you had to look towards Europe. On the west coast of America, and in Hollywood in particular, cars such as British Jaguars and Italian Ferraris were becoming very popular with celebrities of the period. The family man might not be able to afford such exotic machines, but the high-profile display of imported cars among the film star fraternity must have helped break down resistance to buying a foreign car.

VWoA Is Born

Unfortunately, Will Van de Kamp's runaway enthusiasm for the Beetle and the sales network was his undoing. In Nordhoff's eyes, Van de Kamp made the mistake of considering the American market as belonging to him, rather than to Volkswagen. As the eastern dealer network became more efficient, there was less call for a trouble-shooter, or for someone to set up new outlets. Van de Kamp's success was ultimately his downfall when, in April 1955, Volkswagen of America was set up

Above: Manuel Hinke, along with Carl Hahn, was responsible for redesigning the American sales network, in the wake of Van de Kamp.

Below: The Beetle soon proved itself in all conditions in the USA and Canada. Snow presented few problems to the trusty VW.

Right: For many Americans, the first experience of the Volkswagen was gained in Germany while serving with the armed forces towards the

end of the war. Volkswagens, whether requisitioned Beetle sedans or old Kübelwagens such as this, soon earned a lot of respect from the GIs.

to take direct control of the US market, and Carl Hahn was appointed Van de Kamp's successor. However, his undeniable talents did not go to waste as he continued to be involved with one of the many VW agencies he had helped to get started.

Hahn's instruction from Wolfsburg's General Director was to appoint further dealerships but, this time, to concentrate on enlisting the support of those who wished to have sole agencies, i.e., dealerships which only offered Volkswagens for sale – previ-ously, most Volkswagen dealers also sold what might have been considered rival products. Nordhoff had other ideas up his sleeve, too. He felt that Carl Hahn should target people who previously did not even sell cars of any sort, let alone rivals, suggesting that the best existing operations had probably already been picked by American manufacturers.

Hahn placed an even greater emphasis on service back-up than had Van de Kamp, capitalizing on the fact that many other imported cars, and especially those from Great Britain, let their customers down in this vital area. One of the first changes that Hahn and Volkswagen's export chief, Manuel Hinke, carried out was to redesign the American sales network and, in its place, to set up a single sales operation which would gradually lessen the importance placed on the west coast. Thanks to the determination of Nordhoff, Hahn and Hinke to conquer the US market, Volkswagen of America went from strength to strength, impressing customers with its excellent sales and service network.

Although a cabriolet version of the People's Car had been part of the grand plan from day one, it was not until 1949 that official blessing was given to go ahead with production. The company chosen to carry out the assembly of the cabriolet was Wilhelm Karmann in Osnabrück, a long-established, family-run coachbuilding concern. The result was a beautifully-proportioned convertible which bore a close resemblance to the pre-war VW38 prototype in which Hitler rode at the cornerstone ceremony of 1938. Today, early cabriolet Beetles are among the most sought-after of all VWs and, looking at this fine example, it is not too hard to see why.

SPECIFICATIONS

Engine: Horizontally opposed, air-cooled four cylinder. **Construction:** Two-piece cast Elektron alloy crankcase split vertically with separate cast-iron cylinders and cast aluminum alloy pistons. Four main bearings. Cast aluminum cylinder heads with siamesed inlet ports. **Bore and stroke:** 77mm x 64mm. **Capacity:** 1192cc (72ci). **Valves:** Pushrod operated overhead. **Compression ratio:** 6.6:1. **Fuel system:** Mechanical fuel pump; single Solex 26PCI carburetor. **Maximum power:** 30bhp (36 US hp) at 3,700rpm. **Maximum torque:** 56lb ft at 2,000rpm.

Transmission: Four-speed manual transaxle with integral final drive unit. Synchromesh on top three gears only. Two-piece casing. **Gear ratios:** First – 3.60; second – 2.07; third – 1.25; fourth – 0.80; reverse – 6.60. **Final drive ratio:** 4.43:1.

Brakes: Hydraulically-operated drums on all four wheels

Steering: Worm and nut

Suspension: Front: Fully independent with transverse, multi-leaf torsion bars and telescopic dampers. King- and link-pin design. **Rear:** Fully independent swing-axle with twin solid torsion bars and telescopic dampers.

Wheels and tires: 4J x 15in pressed steel wheels. 5.60 x 15 cross-ply tires.

Dimensions: Length: 4070mm (13ft 4.2in). **Width:** 1540mm (5ft 0.6in). **Height:** 1500mm (4ft 11in). **Wheelbase:** 2400mm (7ft 10.5in). **Dry weight:** 780kg (1720lb).

Peformance: Maximum speed: 113km/h (70mph). **Acceleration:** 0-96km/h (60mph): 28sec. **Fuel consumption:** 8.2lts/100km (34.4mpg).

Number built: (1956) 6,550

Owner: Charles Oldroyd

Above: The luggage area changed little in the 1950s, only the gas tank being reshaped to improve luggage space. Whitewall tires were popular, especially in the USA.

Above: Production cabriolets had the engine intake louvers stamped into the deck lid, rather than under the rear window, as on sedans. The folding top of these Karmann-built VWs was of exceptional quality.

Below: The flat shape of the cabrio windshield was retained, giving it a distinctive appearance.

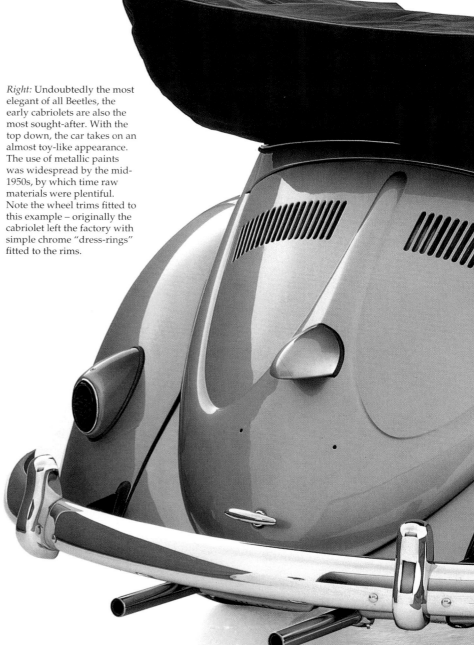

Right: Undoubtedly the most elegant of all Beetles, the early cabriolets are also the most sought-after. With the top down, the car takes on an almost toy-like appearance. The use of metallic paints was widespread by the mid-1950s, by which time raw materials were plentiful. Note the wheel trims fitted to this example – originally the cabriolet left the factory with simple chrome "dress-rings" fitted to the rims.

Above: The dashboard was the same as that of the sedan models. Note the accessory Dehne fuel gauge fitted to the left of the speedometer. A fuel tap was still fitted as standard, located on the floor.

Left: On cabriolet models, the semaphore turn signals were to be found on the rear quarter-panels just behind the doors, making them difficult for other road users to see.

Right: Even with the top up, the Karmann-built cabriolets were as quiet and draft-free as a sedan. Note the more efficient exhaust system with twin exhaust tailpipes which was first fitted in 1954.

Above: The rear side windows could be wound down into the quarter-panels. Note how the chrome-framed window pivots down at an angle.

Right: The cabriolet relied on precisely the same running gear as the sedan model, which, in this instance, included the 36hp, 1192cc engine and four-speed, part-synchromesh transmission.

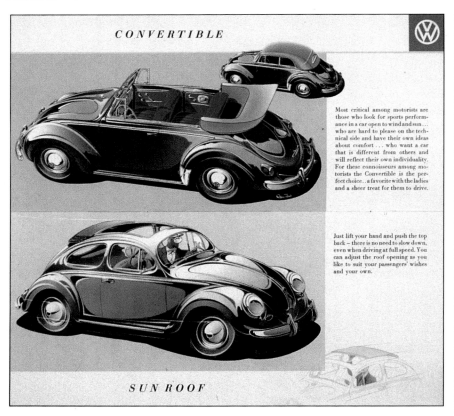

CONVERTIBLE

Most critical among motorists are those who look for sports perform-ance in a car open to wind and sun... who are hard to please on the tech-nical side and have their own ideas about comfort... who want a car that is different from others and will reflect their own individuality. For these connoisseurs among mo-torists the Convertible is the per-fect choice.. a favorite with the ladies and a sheer treat for them to drive.

Just lift your hand and push the top back – there is no need to slow down, even when driving at full speed. You can adjust the roof opening as you like to suit your passengers' wishes and your own.

SUN ROOF

SEDAN
STANDARD AND DE LUXE MODELS

Do you like the European look in automobiles? Are you fond of clean-cut stream-lined cars? Are you keen on riding in easy comfort, yet would like to have a means of trans-portation that is downright cheap to operate? If such is the case, the Volkswagen, the leading European car in its field, is exactly what you are looking for. Technicians the world over say that the Volkswagen is the most sensible automobile ever built and that it is years ahead in design. The Volks-wagen was designed by a genius as unique in his field as Caruso was as a tenor. The Volkswagen Sedan is built in two models, Standard and De Luxe. Both models are handsome in their shining metallic finish. The De Luxe Sedan offers a choice of bewitching colors. Expensive upholstery and handsome practical fittings blend into a harmonious whole with typical European discre-tion. All Volkswagen models offer the same basic fea-tures that make Volkswagens so outstanding. All have that surprisingly fast getaway, that smooth and safe driving thanks to marvelous suspension and a low center of gravity, and that extraordinary economy of opera-tion combined with great driving comfort which charac-terize the Volkswagen and make it unequalled in its field.

Success Story

A measure of its .success throughout the 1950s can be seen from studying a table of US registrations between 1949, when Ben Pon first made his appearance aboard the *Westerdam*, and 1960. Export efforts were very much concentrated on the USA in order to raise much-needed dollars.

Year	VWs registered
1949	2
1950	157
1951	390
1952	611
1953	1,013
1954	6,614
1955	30,928
1956	55,690
1957	79,524
1958	104,306
1959	150,601
1960	191,372

It is interesting to compare these figures with German sales and total worldwide pro-duction over a similar period:

Year	German sales (worldwide production)
1950	50,562 (81,779)
1951	58,469 (93,709)
1952	71,440 (114,348)
1953	89,157 (151,323)
1954	113,169 (202,174)
1955	128,687 (279,986)
1956	141,979 (333,190)
1957	160,781 (380,561)
1958	186,014 (451,526)
1959	228,234 (575,407)

Above: Fresh-air motoring, Volkswagen-style. This 1956 brochure shows the two ways in which a Beetle owner could choose to enjoy a hot summer's day.

Right: The advertising brochures produced during the 1950s have become extremely collectable. The artwork, by Reuters, showed the Beetle in a highly stylized form, making it appear longer and lower than it really was.

However, none of the foregoing quite explains why the Volkswagen Beetle (or "Bug" as it was affectionately known in the USA) should have become such a successful product on the American market. After all, with cheap and plentiful gas, a freeway net-work that was the envy of the world and relatively traffic-free roads, it could be argued that there was no need for a small, fuel-effi-cient car. Already by the mid-1950s, though, there was a growing body of technically-aware people for whom the regular American cars with their huge fins and vast expanses of chrome were of little interest. Some people simply appreciated the finer points of the Volkswagen engineering while others regarded the Volkswagen as a basic form of transport that allowed them to stand out from the crowd. For many, the fascination with the VW was a result of a thrifty, "waste not, want not," outlook, or in many cases it was simply because a parent owned a Beetle which was handed down from father – or, more fre-quently, mother – to son or daughter.

There are many stories of how people were won over to the VW way of life, such as that told by Gene Berg, one of the founding fathers of the Volkswagen performance industry in the USA. His introduction to the Volkswagen was due to an uncle who owned a 1955 model. At the time, Gene was typical of many carefree Americans, driving a 1940 Ford coupé with a tuned flathead V8 engine. However, the fact that his uncle's little Volkswagen could drive along muddy tracks in conditions so bad that a person could hardly stand, let alone walk, made a huge impression. When Gene got mar-ried a year or two later and needed economical transport, he ordered himself a Beetle. He always clearly remembered the cost of that new, black Volkswagen sedan: $1,680, or roughly a dollar per pound in weight.

Many other Americans had developed a familiarity with the Volkswagen while serv-ing with the Army in Germany, either during or immediately after World War II. In the months following the end of hostilities, the only means of transport available to the GIs,

SUN ROOF

Volkswagen Sedans offer a pleasant surprise when they are equipped with a Golde Sun Roof. With a sweep of the hand you can fold the top back and enjoy the fresh air and sunshine. With the Sun Roof closed, the car is just as weatherproof in bad weather as if it had a steel top. All Volkswagen models have ventilator wings in the windows for draftless ventilation.

CONVERTIBLE

If you like to drive a sporty car and enjoy sunshine to the full, the Volkswagen Convertible is the car for you. Wherever you drive or park a Volkswagen Convertible, it attracts the admiring attention of all eyes. Volkswagen has built in the Convertible the car of your dreams. Like all other Volkswagen models, the Convertible has no waste space or superfluous weight. Not an inch of space is unexploited and every ounce of weight is put to good use. The Convertible is the fastest and easiest handling car in turbulent city traffic. Put the top up on a Convertible and you can drive through a cloudburst in comfort. It is absolutely impervious to rain, wind, dust and cold. — It is hard to talk a woman into a Sedan when she has once seen the graceful lines of the Convertible (body by Karmann).

Lemon.

This Volkswagen missed the boat.

The chrome strip on the glove compartment is blemished and must be replaced. Chances are you wouldn't have noticed it; Inspector Kurt Kroner did.

There are 3,389 men at our Wolfsburg factory with only one job: to inspect Volkswagens at each stage of production. (3000 Volkswagens are produced daily; there are more inspectors than cars.)

Every shock absorber is tested (spot checking won't do), every windshield is scanned. Volkswagens have been rejected for surface scratches barely visible to the eye.

Final inspection is really something! VW inspectors run each car off the line onto the Funktionsprüfstand (car test stand), tote up 189 check points, gun ahead to the automatic brake stand, and say "no" to one VW out of fifty. This preoccupation with detail means the VW lasts longer and requires less maintenance, by and large, than other cars. (It also means a used VW depreciates less than any other car.)

Volkswagen plucks the lemons; you get the plums.

Above: The advertising campaign of Doyle, Dane, Bernbach became a classic. Their self-deprecating adverts appeared to poke fun at the Beetle, but the story lines got the desired message across. The "Lemon" advertisement is regarded as one of the best.

Below: The Beetle continued to win respect the world over for its ruggedness and reliability. In Scandinavia, it proved popular for rallying.

other than the worn-out military vehicles, were Volkswagens that had been abandoned by the retreating German Army. More often than not, these were Type 82 Kübelwagens which, of course, used essentially the same engine and running gear as the early Beetles. When the German economy eventually recovered following the currency reform, Volkswagens were virtually the only form of private transportation available. It is, therefore, unsurprising that many American soldiers would have become familiar with the sight of the VW, while many of them would have owned one during their service there.

Although Volkswagen did not officially export Beetles to America until the early 1950s, a number of cars are known to have found their way "home" courtesy of soldiers returning to the USA – they made practical souvenirs of their owner's time spent in Europe! Almost everyone who came into contact with the VW under those circumstances came away impressed with the way it could cope with even the most ham-fisted attempts

Throughout the 1950s, the Beetle was progressively improved in an effort to keep up with rival products. One of the major criticisms of the older models had been poor rearward visibility so, in 1953, Volkswagen enlarged the rear window to produce the familiar "oval-window" model which remained in production until August 1957. Outside Europe, the Beetle continued to sell well, even in the USA where people were used to driving far larger cars. However, to meet increasingly strict regulations, in 1956 VW was forced to abandon the old semapahore turn signals on cars destined for North America, opting instead to fit new flashing turn signals.

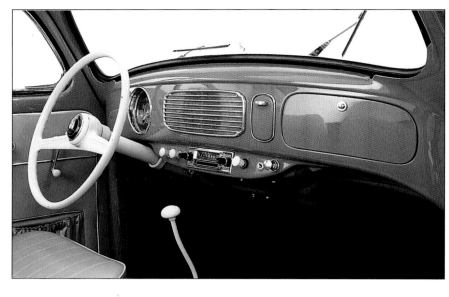

Left: Even for the export markets, the engine specification remained the same. The transmission, however, featured synchromesh on the top three gears, whereas the standard model lacked any synchromesh on any gear.

Above: The dashboards of left- and right-hand drive models were virtual mirror-images of each other, with the speedometer and glove box swapping place according to the position of the steering wheel.

Left: Vinyl interior trim proved to be far more durable than earlier cloth. Simple chrome trim added a touch of sparkle to the austere door panels.

Above: To meet with new American safety regulations, from 1956 onwards Beetles destined for the USA were equipped with "towel-rail" bumper guards – secondary tubular bumpers positioned above the originals.

Above: At the rear, the US-specification bumper guards were of a split design to allow the deck lid to be opened. Note, however, how the new guards partly obscured the already inadequate rear lights.

Left: The most noteworthy change made for the US market was the elimination of the semaphore turn signals in favor of wing-mounted flashing signals. These small bullet-like lights are unique to US-spec vehicles of the late 1950s. The lack of semaphores meant a redesigned door pillar for this one market.

Above: The interior light of oval-window models was located on the cant rail inside the car, above the door. Note the passenger grab strap – a useful standard fitment.

Left: The US-specification rear light incorporated the flashing turn signal – the brake light actually flashed. This style of light was not used in other markets until 1960 when flashing turn signals became universal.

SPECIFICATIONS

Engine: Horizontally opposed, air-cooled four cylinder. **Construction:** Two-piece cast Elektron alloy crankcase split vertically with separate cast-iron cylinders and cast aluminum alloy pistons. Four main bearings. Cast aluminum cylinder heads with siamesed inlet ports. **Bore and stroke:** 77mm x 64mm. **Capacity:** 1192cc (72ci). **Valves:** Pushrod operated overhead. **Compression ratio:** 6.6:1. **Fuel system:** Mechanical fuel pump; single Solex 26PCI carburetor. **Maximum power:** 30bhp (36 US hp) at 3,700rpm. **Maximum torque:** 56lb ft at 2,000rpm.

Transmission: Four-speed manual transaxle with integral final drive unit. Synchromesh on top three gears only. Two-piece casing. **Gear ratios:** First – 3.60; second – 2.07; third – 1.25; fourth – 0.80; reverse – 6.60. **Final drive ratio:** 4.43:1.

Brakes: Hydraulically-operated drums on all four wheels

Steering: Worm and nut

Suspension: Front: Fully independent with transverse, multi-leaf torsion bars and telescopic dampers. King- and link-pin design. **Rear:** Fully independent swing-axle with twin solid torsion bars and telescopic dampers.

Wheels and tires: 4J x 15in pressed steel wheels. 5.60 x 15 cross-ply tires.

Dimensions: Length: 4070mm (13ft 4.2in). **Width:** 1540mm (5ft 0.6in). **Height:** 1500mm (4ft 11in). **Wheelbase:** 2400mm (7ft 10.5in). **Dry weight:** 780kg (1720lb).

Peformance: Maximum speed: 113km/h (70mph). **Acceleration: 0-96km/h (60mph):** 28sec. **Fuel consumption:** 8.2lts/100km (34.4mpg).

Number built: (1957) 380,561

Owner: Glen Illsley

Right: The driver's door lock remained the only one which could be locked or unlocked with a key from outside the vehicle.

by military personnel to maintain the cars
with the minimum of loving care, or to drive
them into the ground, safe in the knowledge
that a replacement would not be far away. In
many ways, the situation was reminiscent of
the pre-war test program, whereby the VW30
prototypes were driven mercilessly by members of the German Army in an attempt to find
the vehicle's weak points.

Classic Advertising

Tales of the car's indestructibility and character grew by the day. Hundreds of jokes were
circulated about the Beetle – how they are so
unreliable you have to carry a spare motor in
the trunk, for example – but they all helped to
enhance the car's mystique. The master stroke
was when, in 1959, the Doyle, Dane, Bernbach
advertising agency was given the contract to
promote Volkswagen in America. Once the
campaign got under way, there seemed to be
no looking back, for instead of ignoring the
jokes, Doyle, Dane, Bernbach turned them to
VW's advantage. DDB made no attempt to
pretty the car up, by making it look more
glamorous or implying it was bigger than it
really was. Most rival car advertising at the
time (and since) consistently made claims that
were hard to swallow.

While many others used air-brushed illustrations to display their vehicles, Volkswagen's agency chose to use real photographs, frequently of older, used models to
impress on the customer that the Beetle was
not just another part of America's throw-away
society. "What you see is what you get" could
have been the VW motto. The Doyle, Dane,
Bernbach campaign rapidly became part of
Volkswagen folklore, with many of the press
advertisements becoming an art-form all of
their own. Several have become classics such
as the famous "Lemon" ad of 1960, which
spoke of Volkswagen's stringent quality control system, or the later "Think Small"
campaign which told of the economical nature
of the VW. Every DDB advert helped to create
an image of reliability, individuality and value
for money that set Volkswagen's Beetle apart
from the Detroit mainstream.

The specification and design of the Beetle
changed quite noticeably throughout the
1950s, although it never lost its basic character.
By 1950, the Beetle had become only slightly
more sophisticated than the first KdF-Wagens
that had appeared a little over ten years
earlier. At the front of the car, Porsche's torsion bar suspension was still in use, consisting
of two sets of multi-leaf torsion bars housed in
a pair of transverse axle tubes. Drum brakes
were used, operated by a system of rods and
cables. At the rear, a pair of torsion bars were
connected to trailing arms which, in turn,
located on the outer end of the swing-axle

Left: The 36hp Volkswagen engine was superbly reliable but costly to build, as it required several complex machining operations during the course of its manufacture.

Right: The 1950s began with the Beetle looking little different to the first post-war products. However, within a decade, the appearance of the Beetle would change significantly as Volkswagen pursued a path of relentless improvement.

Below left: Throughout the 1950s, Heinz Nordhoff placed a great deal of emphasis on the export market, exhibiting at most major motor shows. This was the impressive VW stand at the 1951 Berlin show.

Left: The first sign that changes were afoot was when the 1953 model appeared, with a new dashboard, extra trim and several other significant changes to its specification.

Below: Rometsch was just one of many coachbuilding companies in the 1950s which chose to build a stylish sports car based on the humble Beetle.

driveshafts. Cable-operated drum brakes were to be found here also. The front dampers were conventional telescopic hydraulic units, but those at the rear were of the older-style lever-arm design.

The chassis itself closely resembled the flat floorpan favored by Porsche, although more strengthening ribs were used to increase rigidity. Rear-seat passengers would have approved of the improvement in leg room,

By far the biggest change yet seen in Volkswagen styling occurred when the decision was made, in August 1957, to enlarge the rear window of the Type 1 models. The result was a vehicle which was far more practical to use on the increasingly busy roads of Europe and North America. Introduced at the same time as this redesign was a new dashboard layout which would remain in use, virtually unchanged, until the 1970s. Vehicles of this era were a curious mix of old and new, retaining the old 1192cc engine, first introduced in 1954, along with semaphores and the early-style steering wheel. However, further changes were on the horizon.

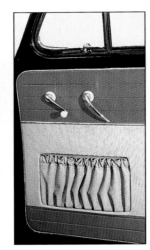

Above: The luggage area of the Beetle had increased only slightly throughout the 1950s and remained woefully small compared with rival products. The gas tank and spare wheel took up a lot of useful space.

Left: The interior trim was much the same as it had been: adequate but not exciting is probably the best way to describe it. A map pocket in the driver's door panel was a useful touch – interior storage would always be at a premium.

Above: The new shape deck lid and larger rear window completely transformed the back view of the Beetle. Other details, however, such as the simple rear lights and bumpers, were unchanged and would remain so for a little while longer.

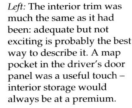

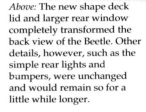

Above: The hand brake and gearshift levers were still located between the front seats. Note the small white heater knob – winding it clockwise would turn the heater on.

SPECIFICATIONS

Engine: Horizontally opposed, air-cooled four cylinder. **Construction:** Two-piece cast Elektron alloy crankcase split vertically with separate cast-iron cylinders and cast aluminum alloy pistons. Four main bearings. Cast aluminum cylinder heads with siamesed inlet ports. **Bore and stroke:** 77mm x 64mm. **Capacity:** 1192cc (72ci). **Valves:** Pushrod operated overhead. **Compression ratio:** 6.6:1. **Fuel system:** Mechanical fuel pump; single Solex 26PCI carburetor. **Maximum power:** 30bhp (36 US hp) at 3,700rpm. **Maximum torque:** 56 lb ft at 2,000rpm.

Transmission: Four-speed manual transaxle with integral final drive unit. Synchromesh on top three gears only. Two-piece casing. **Gear ratios:** First – 3.60; second – 2.07; third – 1.25; fourth – 0.80; reverse – 6.60. **Final drive ratio:** 4.43:1.

Brakes: Hydraulically-operated drums on all four wheels

Steering: Worm and nut

Suspension: Front: Fully independent with transverse, multi-leaf torsion bars and telescopic dampers. King- and link-pin design. **Rear:** Fully independent swing-axle with twin solid torsion bars and telescopic dampers.

Wheels and tires: 4J x 15in pressed steel wheels. 5.60 x 15 cross-ply tires.

Dimensions: Length: 4070mm (13ft 4.2in). **Width:** 1540mm (5ft 0.6in). **Height:** 1500mm (4ft 11in). **Wheelbase:** 2400mm (7ft 10.5in). **Dry weight:** 780kg (1720lb).

Peformance: Maximum speed: 113km/h (70mph). **Acceleration:** 0-96km/h (60mph): 28sec. **Fuel consumption:** 8.2lts/100km (34.4mpg).

Number built: (1959) 575,407

Owner: Peter Younger

Above: The engine still remained the same: 36hp from 1192cc. By now, the writing was on the wall for this venerable unit and a new, more powerful, engine was just around the corner. Likewise, the transmission remained unchanged.

Right: Great news for Volkswagen owners was the introduction of the larger rear window in August 1957. This single change made a significant difference to the appeal of the Beetle in days when traffic volume was increasing rapidly. Note the redesigned deck lid, too. Mudflaps were popular – and practical – accessories, helping to protect the underside of the vehicle from damage by stones.

Above: The big news for 1958 was the new dashboard which was radically different from that of the old oval-window models. This design would remain in use, virtually unaltered, until the 1970s when safety laws dictated a fresh look.

Above: If you ignore the rear window, there appears to be little different about the front of a 1959 Beetle compared with the older oval-window models. However, the windshield is a little deeper.

Above: The semaphores were phased out at the end of the 1950s, and flashing turn signals became standard.

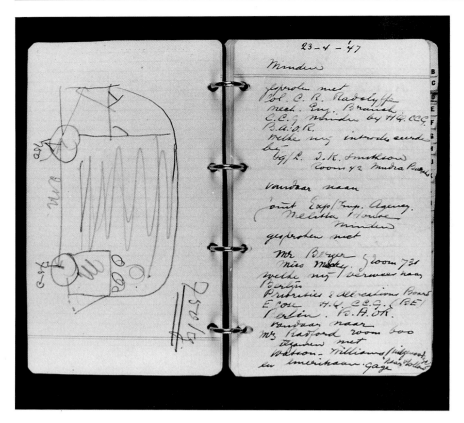

windows rolled up, the car soon became stuffy, a situation made worse when the heater was used. Volkswagen overcame this problem, to a degree, in 1950 when it added small cut-outs to the leading edge of the door glass, allowing fresh, draft-free air into the car simply by winding the window down very slightly. The following year, small opening vents were added to the front quarter panels ahead of the doors which ducted air into the car from below the dashboard. However, this system lasted for less than two years as it proved to be very drafty, earning the vents the nickname of "crotch coolers" in the USA as the fresh air was directed where the occupants least appreciated it!

In the early 1950s, two significant improvements to the car were the change to hydraulic brakes on all export models in 1950 and the use of telescopic rear dampers in 1951. Between them, these two improvements made what was already becoming a good car an

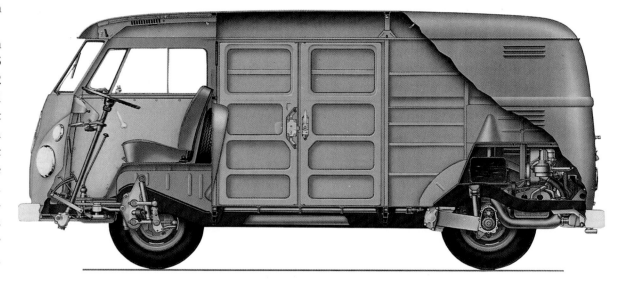

brought about by lowering the floorpan behind the front seats.

Mechanically, the new decade began with the Beetle making use of the 1131cc, 31hp (25 bhp) unit, first introduced in the Type 82 Kübelwagen back in 1943. The engine had proved itself to be extremely reliable, if not over-powerful, and Nordhoff saw no reason why the unit should be changed. He felt that efforts should be directed towards making the car a better product in terms of finish and overall specification. Similarly, the transmission was very much like that used in previous years, although the casing was now ribbed for greater strength, unlike the smoother design seen on the KdF-Wagen.

Constant Change

In July 1949, Volkswagen had introduced an "export" version of the Beetle, which was designed to appeal to foreign markets where there was greater competition from rival products. These export-specification cars came with chromed hubcaps, door handles, headlamp rims and bumpers, polished aluminum body trim and a new two-spoke ivory-colored steering wheel which replaced the black, three-spoke design of the standard model. While the standard model came in semi-gloss grey paint, the export VW could be had in a range of high-gloss colors including green, blue, red, beige and black. Inside the export model, the interior trim was of a higher quality while the dashboard now featured a removable panel to the right of the speedometer to allow a clock to be fitted.

One problem that had come to light, particularly in cold climates, was the lack of adequate ventilation in the Beetle. With the

Left: The Type 2 lent itself to being signwritten; its large, flat body panels were a publicist's delight.

Right: The 23-window Deluxe model was popular with hotels and schools as it could carry up to nine people with ease.

Below left: A line-up of very early Type 2s – note the lack of rear windows.

Below right: An ambulance conversion was one of many offered by the factory.

even better one. The standard model was forced to soldier on with the dreadfully antiquated cable-brake system, however, and owners had to prepare themselves for the brakes to lock on in very cold weather as the cables became frozen in their guides.

Out With The Old

The next, and arguably the most noticeable, stage in the Beetle's development took place in 1953 when the split rear window, which had been part of the Beetle's design since the KdF prototypes, made way for a single oval-shaped window which offered some 23 per cent greater area. With this, and a dashboard that had been radically redesigned the previous year, the Beetle took on a considerably more modern appearance. The only drawback to this redesign (at least, as far as future collectors and restorers were concerned) was that a small industry sprung up with several workshops offering to cut the central dividing bar out of the old split-window cars to mimic the

new look! Export models also benefited from synchromesh being incorporated on the top three gears in the transmission, making the Beetle far more pleasant to drive. As far as the factory was concerned, the greatest news was that the 500,000th Beetle finally rolled off the assembly line on July 3rd, 1953. The Volkswagen was here to stay.

The trusty 1131cc, 31hp engine, which had provided the motivation behind the Kübelwagen, Schwimmwagen and the first production Beetles, was finally redesigned for 1954 and grew to 1192cc and 36hp. This engine, although of essentially the same layout as its predecessor, allowed the Beetle to cruise at between 8 and 16km/h (5 and 10mph) faster and proved to be one of the most reliable engines ever built by Volkswagen. As a measure of its success, the same engine remained in production until the end of the decade, seeing service in all Volkswagen models. Even as late as the 1960s, the engine was available in the standard sedan

and was still popular for such applications as fire-pumps and generators.

On August 5th, 1955, the 1,000,000th Beetle was produced at Wolfsburg, a milestone which Heinz Nordhoff celebrated by announcing a cut in the purchase price. The Standard model was cut from DM3,950 to DM3,790, the Export from DM4,850 to DM4,700 and the cabriolet from DM6,500 to DM5,990. Throughout the year, several improvements were made to the car, including the fitting of flashing turn signals for the American market in place of the traditional semaphores. Surprisingly, the cars produced for other markets, including Germany, retained the out-dated mechanical turn signals which, as always, were mounted in the door "B" pillar. US-specification models also gained the unwieldy "towel rail" bumper guards which were designed to bring the VW's bumper height up to something closer to that of the average domestic US car. Both of these modifications were introduced in

The Dutchman, Ben Pon, is credited with being the person responsible for persuading the factory to produce a small commercial vehicle based on the mechanical components of the Type 1 sedan. He realized that there was an increasing number of small businessmen who were in desperate need of a delivery vehicle which offered the reliability of a Volkswagen sedan, yet which would be capable of carrying a higher payload. The result was the box-like Type 2, the first new design to come from the factory since the war. With its compact dimensions and heavy-duty suspension, this new VW proved to be far superior to its many contemporary rivals.

Left: There was no shortage of seating in Volkswagen's people-carrier. Three rows of seats enabled up to eight or nine people to be carried with ease. The large window area gave the interior a light and airy feeling.

Above: The dashboard of the early Type 2 was reminiscent of that of the contemporary Beetle – indeed, the two vehicles shared the same instrument panels. Note, however, that the Type 2 has three panels, the center one frequently being fitted with a radio, while a clock appeared on the oposite side to the speedometer.

MFF 692

SPECIFICATIONS

Engine: Horizontally opposed, air-cooled four cylinder. **Construction:** Two-piece cast Elektron alloy crankcase split vertically with separate cast-iron cylinders and cast aluminum alloy pistons. Four main bearings. Cast aluminum cylinder heads with siamesed inlet ports. **Bore and stroke:** 77mm x 64mm. **Capacity:** 1192cc (72ci). **Valves:** Pushrod operated overhead. **Compression ratio:** 5.8:1. **Fuel system:** Mechanical fuel pump; single Solex 26VFJ carburetor. **Maximum power:** 30bhp (36 US hp) at 3,300rpm. **Maximum torque:** 56lb ft at 2,000rpm.

Transmission: Four-speed manual, non-synchromesh transaxle with integral final drive unit. Two-piece casing. **Gear ratios:** First – 3.60; second – 2.07; third – 1.25; fourth – 0.80; reverse – 6.60. **Final drive ratio:** 4.43:1. **Reduction gear ratio:** 1.4:1

Brakes: Hydraulically-operated drums on all four wheels

Steering: Worm and nut

Suspension: Front: Fully independent with transverse, multi-leaf torsion bars and telescopic dampers. King- and link-pin design. **Rear:** Fully independent swing-axle with twin solid torsion bars and telescopic dampers. Reduction gears on rear axles.

Wheels and tires: 4J x 16in pressed steel wheels. 5.20 x 16 cross-ply tires.

Dimensions: Length: 4191mm (13ft 9in). **Width:** 1702mm (5ft 7.1in). **Height:** 1941mm (6ft 4.4in). **Wheelbase:** 2400mm (7ft 10.5in). **Dry weight:** 1103kg (2432lb).

Peformance: Maximum speed: 95km/h (59mph). **Acceleration:** 0-80km/h (50mph): 30.6sec. **Fuel consumption:** 9.44lts/100km (28.7mpg).

Number built: (1950-1967) c1,800,000

Owner: Richard King

Above: Due to the different driving position, the Type 2's gearshift lever was much longer than the Beetle's and the emergency (hand) brake lever was vertical. Note flat floor to the cab.

Below: Type 2s were equipped with semaphore turn signals up until 1960 when flashing turn signals were first introduced. Semaphores were located on the door pillars.

Above: Early models were nicknamed "barn door" Type 2s because of the large, hinged engine access panel at the back. The small light in the center is the brake warning lamp. Note the tiny rear lights and the rudimentary bumpers which would have offered little in the way of protection in the event of a crash.

Left: Originally conceived by Ben Pon, the Dutch importer of Volkswagens, the Type 2 was a success story from the very beginning. Based largely on Beetle mechanical components (engine and transmission), the Type 2 featured heavy-duty front suspension and an increased ride height due to reduction gears on the rear axles. This stunning Samba model was the top of the range, with extra trim, two-color paint and roof-mounted windows. The paint scheme of Chestnut Brown and Sealing Wax Red is particularly attractive.

Left: The de luxe Samba models were all equipped with this full-length sun-roof, a feature which was to prove especially popular in hot climates.

Right: The Beetle's trusty 36hp, 1192cc engine was called into play in the Type 2, meaning that performance was best described as adequate, but never exciting.

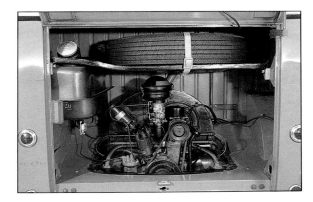

Left: First launched in 1955, the Karmann Ghia was the odd-one-out in the Volkswagen range. Up to that point, VW had only offered thoroughly practical vehicles with few frills: the Beetle and the Type 2.

Below: Undoubtedly attractive, especially in this color combination, the Ghia was a hit right from the start – notably in the US market. It is not difficult to understand why.

August 1955 in readiness for cars that were to be released in the 1956 model year.

The Beetle remained virtually unchanged until August 1957 when the rear window was enlarged by a massive 95 per cent, while the windshield grew by 17 per cent. The result was a car which felt altogether far less claustrophobic than previous years' models. At the rear, the appearance of the deck lid was substantially changed for the first time since the KdF-Wagen appeared. The familiar "W" design with its strongly defined swage lines gave way to a smoother, simpler deck lid which was to see service virtually unchanged for another ten years. Inside the car, the dashboard was totally redesigned, too, with a larger glovebox, provisions for a radio in the center of the panel and grilles either side of the speedometer, one of which could house an optional loudspeaker.

The Beetle remained in essentially this form for the remainder of the decade, but it is worth noting that it was no longer the only product being offered by Volkswagen in the 1950s. In the first year of the new decade, Volkswagen announced a new model known as the Type 2. This was a commercial vehicle based on a sketch made by the indefatigable Ben Pon during a visit to the factory. Pon correctly surmised that there was a need for a reliable commercial vehicle which could be driven and easily maintained by the small businessman. As the German economy was slowly recovering from the ravages of war, many small companies sprang up to capitalize on the new-found wealth. These businesses needed a vehicle which offered the reliability of a Volkswagen yet could cope with carrying a useful payload.

Left: A cabriolet Ghia was first offered in August 1957. The example shown was built after August 1959 – compare the shape of the front fenders and the fresh-air vents with those of the earlier cars opposite.

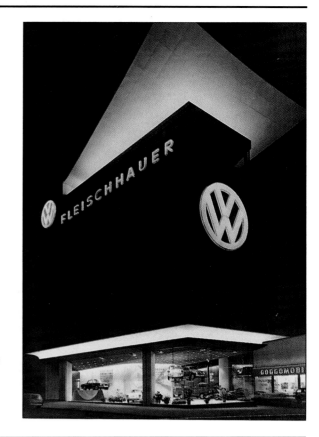

Right: Volkswagen dealerships of the 1950s and '60s had a certain elegance all of their own. They were impressive in the way they promoted the VW image in a stylish manner. Note the Goggomobile dealer to the right – while the VW agency would survive through the 1960s, its rival would not.

New Arrivals

Pon's sketch consisted of a box-like body mounted on what was more or less a Beetle chassis. While this particular layout proved to be impractical – the Beetle floorpan was not strong enough to carry a large load placed in the center – the idea appealed to Nordhoff who gave the go-ahead to design and produce a suitable vehicle. The end result was a simple, one-piece body welded onto a chassis frame which was far stronger than the sedan's floorpan. The trusty 1131cc, 31hp engine was pressed into service, as was the Beetle's transmission – with one notable modification. In order to increase the ground clearance, reduction boxes were fitted to either end of the rear axle shafts in exactly the same way as on the old Type 82 Kübelwagen. At the front, a new, heavy-duty suspension unit was used, based on the design used on passenger cars.

The Type 2, or "Bulli" as it became affectionately known, proved to be a huge success, seeing regular use with all kinds of businesses and even the emergency services. One of the most popular conversions was into the role of ambulance – the factory even offered such a conversion themselves. In later years, the Type 2 would become the mainstay of the mobile home or "camper" market, earning itself an unparalleled reputation for longevity and reliability the world over.

The second new product to appear in the 1950s was the stylish Karmann Ghia, in both coupé and cabriolet form. Following the success of the Karmann-built Beetle cabriolets, consideration was given to producing a somewhat more glamorous model designed to appeal to a wider audience. Wilhelm Karmann had long held a desire to build a sports car of his own and talks took place between the Osnabrück works and Wolfsburg, with a view to producing a Volkswagen-based sports car. Heinz Nordhoff was not particularly interested in the idea as all his thoughts – and the factory's spare capacity – were being taken up with producing the Beetle in sufficient quantities to meet the ever-increasing demand.

Others might have given up at this first hurdle, but Karmann persisted, eventually persuading Nordhoff to allow him to submit some designs. These were duly examined by Ludwig Boehner, head of production development, and Karl Feuereissen, head of the sales and service operation. Both were impressed with the overall concept but remained unmoved by the styling. Karmann turned to the well-established Ghia styling studio in Turin for inspiration and the result was a beautiful, timeless two-seat coupé, the design credits for which have always been hotly contested by both parties.

The Karmann Ghia, as the new car came to be called, was eventually given Nordhoff's blessing and went into production in 1955, to be met with universal praise. In America, the Karmann Ghia became extremely popular, being criticized only for its rather lackluster performance. After all, despite their svelte good looks, the stylish coupé and its cabriolet stable-mate relied only on an unmodified Volkswagen drivetrain.

With the Beetle going from strength to strength, increasing export sales, a successful commercial vehicle and a sports car of its own, Volkswagen could look forward to the next decade with a confidence few other automobile manufacturers could match.

Despite producing the successful cabriolet Beetle for Volkswagen, Wilhelm Karmann had a long-held ambition to build a car of his own, as had Ferdinand Porsche. In the early 1950s, Karmann began negotiations with Volkswagen with a view to producing a sporting vehicle based on VW components. The talks led nowhere so Karmann turned to the Ghia styling studio in Turin, Italy, for inspiration. The result was a wonderfully stylish two-seat coupé and convertible which, in 1955 and following much discussion, eventually gained Heinz Nordhoff's approval. Today, early Karmann Ghias are held in high esteem by Volkswagen enthusiasts.

Left: The engine of the Ghia models was the same as that used in the contemporary sedan, with detail changes to the air-filter to cater for the lower body line. The battery was repositioned to the wider engine bay for greater convenience.

Right: Interior trim of the Karmann Ghia was always better than that of the Beetle. Note the large map pocket in the door panel.

Above: The dashboard was far more stylish than the Beetle's, with extra instrumentation and more trim. The steering wheel was unique to the model and looked far more modern than the sedan's. Note the use of the Wolfsburg city crest in the center of the steering wheel.

Left: The top of the Karmann Ghia cabriolet was extremely well-fitting. Note the finishing strip across the top of it and the small rear window.

SPECIFICATIONS

Engine: Horizontally opposed, air-cooled four cylinder. **Construction:** Two-piece cast Elektron alloy crankcase split vertically with separate cast-iron cylinders and cast aluminum alloy pistons. Four main bearings. Cast aluminum cylinder heads with siamesed inlet ports. **Bore and stroke:** 77mm x 64mm. **Capacity:** 1192cc (72ci). **Valves:** Pushrod operated overhead. **Compression ratio:** 6.6:1. **Fuel system:** Mechanical fuel pump; single Solex 26PCI carburetor. **Maximum power:** 30bhp (36 US hp) at 3,700rpm. **Maximum torque:** 56lb ft at 2,000rpm.

Transmission: Four-speed manual transaxle with integral final drive unit. Synchromesh on top three gears only. Two-piece casing. **Gear ratios:** First – 3.60; second – 2.07; third – 1.25; fourth – 0.80; reverse – 6.60. **Final drive ratio:** 4.43:1.

Brakes: Hydraulically-operated drums on all four wheels

Steering: Worm and nut

Suspension: Front: Fully independent with transverse, multi-leaf torsion bars and telescopic dampers King- and link-pin design. **Rear:** Fully independent swing-axle with twin solid torsion bars and telescopic dampers.

Wheels and tires: 4J x 15in pressed steel wheels. 5.60 x 15 cross-ply tires.

Dimensions: Length: 4140mm (13ft 7in). **Width:** 1620mm (5ft 3.8in). **Height:** 1325mm (4ft 4.2in). **Wheelbase:** 2400mm (7ft 10.5in). **Dry weight:** 798kg (1760lb).

Peformance: Maximum speed: 122km/h (76mph). **Acceleration:** 0-96km/h (60mph): n/a. **Fuel consumption:** 8.2lts/100km (34.4mpg).

Number built: (1955-1974) 363,401

Owner: Derek Frow

Left: The Karmann Ghia wore this unique VW badge on the nose, ahead of the front luggage compartment.

Left: The air intake louvers for the rear-mounted engine were located near the top of the deck lid. Note the very stylish Karmann Ghia script and the small tail light units.

Above: The vents in the front panel are to duct air through to the interior – something the Beetle lacked. Today, early Karmann Ghia bumpers are extremely hard to find in good condition.

Below: Despite the more modern styling, the Ghia lacked luggage space. However, there was extra stowage available behind the front seats as the car was really only a two-seater.

Left: The Karmann Ghia, whether in open cabriolet or closed coupé form, was the most beautiful of all Beetle variations. The result of a three-way marriage between Volkswagen, Karmann, and the Ghia styling studio, it is hard to believe the car is based on the humble Beetle.

If the 1950s saw the Volkswagen Beetle become well and truly established on the world market, then the 1960s would see it undergo several major revisions that were intended to keep it there. The new decade began modestly enough, with Volkswagen making few changes to the car other than detail modifications to the interior – for example, a new steering wheel with semi-circular horn ring for the 1960 models at last replaced the rather dated one that had been in place since the mid-fifties – or adding an anti-roll bar for the front suspension. Probably the most useful change as far as the driver was concerned was the self-cancelling turn signal arm.

The factory, however, saw some rather more important changes taking place, both physically and financially. At long last, and doubtless much to the workers' delight, the last of the old wartime barrack blocks were torn down thereby severing the last of the undesirable links with the VW's occasionally shadowy past. As far as the company's finances were concerned, there had been plentiful discussion about who actually owned the Wolfsburg plant. The state of

Above: Wolfsburg finally shook off the last of the links with its less-illustrious past when the old wartime barracks blocks were torn down. The tall chimneys had, by now, become a familiar landmark, visible for several miles around.

Lower Saxony believed it to belong to its people, while the German government felt it was a national asset. Finally, the problems were resolved when the company was floated on the stock exchange on August 22nd, 1960. However, the government in Bonn retained a

Left: Nordhoff was coming under increasing pressure to expand the model line-up. The Beetle, while still a huge success, was starting to show its age as a design.

Right: On August 22nd, 1960, VW was floated on the German stock exchange, with 60 percent of its shares offered to the public.

Below: The 1960s saw much redevelopment of the factory as new models and increased production put ever-greater pressure on the existing infrastructure.

20 percent stake, with another 20 percent being held by Lower Saxony – the remaining 60 percent was offered to the public to raise further capital.

As a result of this course of action, the Volkswagen purse swelled from DM 300 million in 1959 to around DM 600 million in 1960, providing the factory with the wherewithal to invest in new projects. With 3.6 million shares on offer, there was no shortage of investors at the initial price of DM 50 per share. Just over one year later, Volkswagen announced that the shares had increased in value by around 12 percent, providing a healthy return for those investors who wished to make a quick financial killing.

The other big news, as far as the factory was concerned, was the increase in productivity, with Heinz Nordhoff being able to proudly announce that daily Beetle production had topped the 4,000 mark. However, no matter how many cars Wolfsburg was able to produce, it was still unable to keep up with demand. In 1960, Volkswagen dealers were still having to quote a five-month delivery time for the car, in stark contrast to rivals who could guarantee delivery within a few weeks at the most. Perhaps it was time for Volkswagen to make some big decisions if it was to keep hold of its number one spot in the market place. Nordhoff, for all his leadership qualities, did at times appear to remain complacent about the company's products, giving the impression that the Beetle was all that

Right: Incredible though it may seem, the basic "standard" Beetle was still available in the early 1960s, complete with its cable-operated brakes, early-style steering wheel and total lack of chrome trim.

Below: The 1,000,000th Type 2 – a 23-window Deluxe "Samba" – came off the production line in 1962, some 12 years after the model's introduction. The event was, as always, cause for much celebration.

Volkswagen needed to stay at the top. However, as time would unquestionably prove, appearances can be deceiving.

As a whole, the German motor industry was expanding, with total vehicle production exceeding 2,000,000 units in 1960. As far as Volkswagen was concerned, production reached 725,939 cars – just over 700,000 of which were export models – and some 139,919 Type 2 commercials. The factory's fortunes

continued to improve, with a turnover of some DM 4.6 billion for 1960. In Germany there were now over 1,300 VW dealers, with a further 4,000 to be found overseas. Together they helped to take total sales of the Beetle through the 4,000,000 mark by the end of the calendar year.

There were changes afoot, however. First of all, for 1961, the Beetle engine was at long last redesigned or, more correctly, replaced with a

The 1960s saw many changes in the Beetle's specification and appearance. The 1961 model year had seen the introduction of a new engine, the 1192cc, 40hp unit which would remain in service in German-built Beetles for another 17 years. With this new engine came a redesigned transmission which, however, still lacked synchromesh on first gear. For 1962, the most noticeable change was the installation of new rear lights with separate turn signal lenses for increased safety. Many consider these early 1960s Beetles to be some of the best ever made, with reliable mechanical components and excellent build quality, while still retaining plenty of character.

SPECIFICATIONS

Engine: Horizontally opposed, air-cooled four cylinder. **Construction:** Two-piece cast magnesium-alloy crankcase split vertically with separate cast-iron cylinders and cast aluminum alloy pistons. Four main bearings. Cast aluminum cylinder heads with siamesed inlet ports. **Bore and stroke:** 77mm x 64mm. **Capacity:** 1192cc (69ci). **Valves:** Pushrod operated overhead. **Compression ratio:** 7.0:1. **Fuel system:** Mechanical fuel pump; single Solex 28PICT carburetor. **Maximum power:** 34bhp (40 US hp) at 3,600rpm. **Maximum torque:** 61lb ft at 2,000rpm.

Transmission: Fully-synchromesh, four-speed manual transaxle with integral final drive unit. One-piece casing. **Gear ratios:** First – 3.80; second – 2.06; third – 1.32; fourth – 0.89; reverse – 3.88. **Final drive ratio:** 4.375 :1.

Brakes: Hydraulically-operated drums on all four wheels

Steering: Worm and roller

Suspension: Front: Fully independent with transverse, multi-leaf torsion bars and telescopic dampers. King- and link-pin design with hydraulic steering damper. Rear: Fully independent swing-axle with twin solid torsion bars and telescopic dampers.

Wheels and tires: 4J x 15in pressed steel wheels. 5.60 x 15 cross-ply tires.

Dimensions: Length: 4070mm (13ft 4.2in). **Width:** 1540mm (5ft 0.6in). **Height:** 1500mm (4ft 11in). **Wheelbase:** 2400mm (7ft 10.5in). **Dry weight:** 780kg (1720lb).

Peformance: Maximum speed: 116km/h (72mph). **Acceleration:** 0-96km/h (60mph) c27sec. **Fuel consumption:** 8.1lits/100km (34mpg)

Number built: (1962) 876,255

Owner: Graham Smith

Above right: The dashboard was little changed save for the addition of a fuel gauge. The ignition lock was now located on the steering column. An accessory flower vase was popular, while a spotlight was practical.

Right: The Hazet toolkit contained most items needed to carry out roadside repairs. Today, such kits are highly prized among collectors of Volkswagen accessories.

Right: The door handles were, by now, equipped with push-buttons to open the doors. New door locks were also incorporated in 1961.

Below: The range of colors offered by Volkswagen was large and included many attractive shades. Pastel hues, such as this L380 Turquoise, were popular and suited the lines of the Beetle well. Whitewall tires add the finishing touch, although they were not fitted as standard by the factory. The sun visor over the front windshield is an accessory part, as are the mudflaps and door protectors.

Left: The turn signals were universally mounted on the tops of the front fenders in 1961, the semaphore signals having finally been laid to rest. The design was first seen in the USA in 1958.

Above left & right: The style of the Beetle had progressively changed over the years and, by the early 1960s, its had taken on a refreshing new look. New rear light assemblies incorporated separate turn signal lenses and a new engine cover was introduced to allow space for the larger capacity 1192cc, 40hp engine.

Right: The new engine, first introduced in the Beetle in August 1960 for the 1961 models, was a great improvement on the older 36hp unit. It was not only more powerful but produced more torque. By the end of 1962, a new heating system would be introduced also.

Right: The new tail lights were a considerable improvement, allowing following drivers to see the turn signals more clearly.

version of the new engine introduced on the Type 2 range a year earlier. No longer, except for the fact that it was still an air-cooled flat-four design, could the unit be compared with that first seen in the Kübelwagen and Schwimmwagen back in the 1940s. The new engine shared nothing with its predecessor, other than its capacity: 1192cc. A new crankcase, crankshaft, camshaft, cylinders, pistons, cylinder heads, fuel pump and cooling system all helped make this latest engine a more robust unit which also happened to produce more power: 40hp as opposed to 36hp. Although that may not seem a huge improvement in modern terms, as a percentage it represented an increase of over 13 percent – a useful gain on such a low-power vehicle.

More Changes

In addition to the revised engine, a new transmission made its appearance. This was a totally new design, with a one-piece casing as opposed to the old "split-case" transaxle which had been in use relatively unchanged since the late 1940s. The new transmission benefited from having synchromesh on all forward gears, making it far more pleasant to use, especially in traffic where, on the old model, first gear could only be selected at rest. With a stronger casing, the new design proved to be longer lasting and remained in production, essentially unchanged, until the 1980s.

There were several other modifications made to the Beetle at the same time, including, much to the passenger's delight, the fitting of a second sun visor as standard. The gas tank was also redesigned and, although having a larger capacity, it resulted in an increase in available luggage space under the hood.

In the following year, Volkswagen was somewhat more restrained in its program of continuous improvement, with the biggest news being a redesigned rear-light cluster which now featured a larger lens area with a separate amber turn signal located at the top. The hood finally lost its troublesome over-center stay which had been fitted to all Beetles since the very beginning. This had been the cause of many damaged hoods as gas station attendants tried to shut them without first releasing the stay. A pair of heavy springs now did the job of holding the hood open.

Perhaps the most useful improvement was the fitting of a fuel gauge on the dashboard alongside the speedometer, the old floor-mounted reserve tap at last disappearing – except on the standard models. The latter Beetles were rather idiosyncratic in that they still made use of the old 36hp engine, came with cable-operated brakes and the customary lack of trim. Although not a big seller by this time, the standard model was to remain on offer for several years to come.

Left: In September 1961, VW announced the new Type 3 model, shown here in pre-production form. Based on the mechanical layout of the Beetle, it was a more modern design in every respect.

Above: The Type 3 featured a wider floorpan than that of the Beetle, along with revised front suspension and a new "pancake" engine design which allowed it to fit under a rear luggage area.

Right: The Type 3, shown here in sedan, or "Notchback," form, could never match the sales successes of the Beetle. However, it proved to be an extremely practical design.

The big news, however, was not to do with the Beetle, but a new model called the Type 3. First announced in September 1961, the new car, which would be sold as the VW 1500, appeared to share little with the Beetle. A new engine – again a development of the unit now used in the Type 2 – was all new, with a swept volume of some 1498cc. The body was far more conventional in styling terms (compared with the Beetle, at least), being what is today known as a "three-box" design and came to be nicknamed the "Notchback." Ever ones to prove they knew how to get the most into the least, Wolfsburg's stylists bestowed upon the Type 3 the unique feature of front and rear luggage compartments. To achieve this, the Type 2 engine was redesigned, with a new cooling system that allowed the engine to be fitted under the floor of the rear luggage area, the cooling fan now being driven from the end of the crankshaft rather than off the generator.

The arrival of the Type 3 on the scene was a very timely development, for the Beetle was having trouble maintaining its lead in the sales stakes. Its market share was down by some 8 percent at a time when total vehicle sales in Germany were up by over 10 percent. Although Volkswagen could still boast that it retained a third of the domestic market, out-selling its nearest rival by a factor of two, the overall trend for the company was downward and market share would drop below 30 percent the following year.

One interesting – and troublesome – chapter in Volkswagen's history finally came to a close in October 1961, when a settlement was made

Left: There were several significant features on the new model which would eventually find their way onto the Beetle: flat hubcaps, a larger, 1500cc engine and, eventually, disc brakes. Some called the Type 3 dowdy in its styling but, while undoubtedly plain in appearance, it was a very good product.

Right: The Notchback was joined at its launch by the Variant, or "Squareback." This practical vehicle had a large luggage capacity and was the longest-running Type 3 model of all.

Left: In August 1965, the two other Type 3s were joined by the "Fastback" – a coupé with sporting looks but sedan car performance. A well-proportioned car, it proved to be a popular model in the VW line-up.

to those people who had taken advantage of Hitler's KdF saving scheme over twenty years earlier. The case was first brought to court by a group of savers, led by Karl Stolz, as far back as January 1950. Stolz argued that it was not the fault of those people who had joined the KdF savings scheme that they had lost all their money after the war. He believed, as did his many followers, that Volkswagen had a moral obligation to repay the money in one form or another, either as a direct rebate or in the form of a discount against the purchase of a new Beetle. Volkswagen management maintained that the present company had no connection whatsoever with the pre-war system and could not be held responsible, either morally or legally, for their conduct.

Legal Complications

At the first court hearing, the judge rejected the savers' claim on the basis that the whole KdF scheme had been nothing but Nazi propaganda. The case went before the supreme court and while the decision was not totally reversed, there was the feeling that Volkswagen might be considered a partner to the original scheme. Unsure of what the future might hold, Nordhoff took the bull by the horns and sought a more precise ruling on the case. This time Volkswagen was found to be "guilty" and ordered to pay the court costs.

However, that was not the end of things, for in 1954 more evidence was brought before the court and a judgement made that while Volkswagen was not a partner, it was a responsible party and could therefore be sued by the savers. The following year, the state court then overturned that ruling! The savings group considered whether to accept a compromise when the factory made an offer of DM 250 cash or a credit of DM 500 against the

Above: Such was the esteem in which the Beetle was held that, in 1964, Pope Paul VI blessed a line of Volkswagens destined for the USA! How many other cars can boast such an honor?

Left: This photograph, dated 1960, serves to prove the continuing popularity of the Beetle throughout the developing world. Taken in South America, it shows a Beetle which had been modified for racing.

Right: Nordhoff believed that the reputation of the company stood, or fell, with every car which left the factory. Strict quality inspections were thus carried out at every stage of the production process.

Left: On December 4th, 1961, the 5,000,000th Volkswagen to be built since the end of the war left the assembly line at Wolfsburg. Fewer than four years later, that number would be doubled.

Above: Further proof of VW's continued success on the world market came when Volkswagen of Canada was founded in the early 1960s.
Right: Volkswagen of America's New Jersey HQ.

purchase of a new Beetle. This was turned down and the savers returned to the supreme court, only to have the case referred back to the lower courts once again.

Finally, in 1961, the case came to an end when the courts ruled that Volkswagen should make cash repayments of between DM 25 and DM 100, or a credit of between DM 150 and DM 600 against a new car, depending on how many stamps the saver had in his book. It would be another nine years before the last payments were made, honoring over 120,000 KdF saving contracts, of which just over a half of the claimants opted to buy a new car. The total cost to the company was in excess of DM 34 million, either in cash or credit. The last remaining ghost from the past had finally been laid to rest.

Rising Production

The end of 1962 would see a leap to a production run of some 1,004,338 vehicles, while the 1,000,000th Beetle was sold in the USA. America had become such a large and impor-tant market that Volkswagen opened a new headquarters there, at Englewood Cliffs in New Jersey, on November 20th, 1962. In hindsight it is perhaps a little surprising that the company never opened a manufacturing plant in North America specifically to assemble the Beetle, considering how many of them were sold there. Many years later, a VW plant would be built in Westmoreland, Pennsylvania, to assemble the Rabbit, the US version of the best-selling Golf, but it was destined to close after a troubled history.

If there had been one criticism consistently levelled at the Beetle over the years, it was that it was somewhat underpowered. In the early years this was not a problem as roads were empty and traffic speed low, but as the years passed and roads became more crowded, it became obvious that something would have to be done. VW's solution was to build a 1285cc Beetle fitted with what was essentially a 1200 engine equipped with the crankshaft from the Type 3 model. The bodyshell was also redesigned, with larger glass area all round, resulting in a less gloomy interior and vastly improved visibility. The Beetle was embarking on a period of evolution.

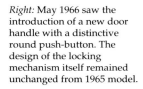

Right: The windshield wipers now parked to the left of the windshield. This was not always popular as it left an unswept area of the windshield in front of the driver. Note how the new, deeper, windshield glass necessitated a redesign of the front scuttle panel.

Right: May 1966 saw the introduction of a new door handle with a distinctive round push-button. The design of the locking mechanism itself remained unchanged from 1965 model.

Below: The door mirror continued to be mounted on the hinge. Only one (on the driver's side) was fitted by the factory – this second mirror is a later addition.

Above: The dashboard remained unchanged with the exception of a center-mounted defroster vent.

Volkswagens always had a poor reputation when it came to keeping the windshield clear of mist and this

expedient was thought to be the cure. Note the half-circle horn ring and the accessory parcel shelf.

Left: A change in the design of the suspension was heralded by the introduction of a new slotted wheel and a redesigned, flatter, hubcap. Wheels were always two-toned like this.

Below: A new locking mechanism prevented the seat backs from tipping forward in the event of an accident – a feature required by increasingly-stringent US safety laws.

SPECIFICATIONS

Engine: Horizontally opposed, air-cooled four cylinder. **Construction:** Two-piece cast magnesium-alloy crankcase split vertically with separate cast-iron cylinders and cast aluminum alloy pistons. Four main bearings. Cast aluminum cylinder heads with siamesed inlet ports. **Bore and stroke:** 77mm x 69mm. **Capacity:** 1285cc (78.4ci). **Valves:** Pushrod operated overhead. **Compression ratio:** 7.3:1. **Fuel system:** Mechanical fuel pump; single Solex 28PICT carburetor. **Maximum power:** 40bhp (50 US hp) at 4,000rpm. **Maximum torque:** 70lb ft at 2,000rpm.

Transmission: Fully-synchromesh, four-speed manual transaxle with integral final drive unit. One-piece casing. **Gear ratios:** First – 3.80; second – 2.06; third – 1.32; fourth – 0.89; reverse – 3.88. **Final drive ratio:** 4.375:1.

Brakes: Hydraulically-operated drums on all four wheels

Steering: Worm and roller

Suspension: Front: Fully independent with transverse, multi-leaf torsion bars and telescopic dampers. Ball-joint design with hydraulic steering damper. **Rear:** Fully independent swing-axle with twin solid torsion bars and telescopic-dampers.

Wheels and tires: 4J x 15in pressed steel wheels. 5.60 x 15 cross-ply tires.

Dimensions: Length: 4237mm (13ft 10.8in). **Width:** 1540mm (5ft 0.6in). **Height:** 1500mm (4ft 11in). **Wheelbase:** 2400mm (7ft 10.5in). **Dry weight:** 780kg (1720lb).

Peformance: Maximum speed: 127km/h (79mph). **Acceleration:** 0-96km/h (60mph): 23sec. **Fuel consumption:** 8.1lits/100km (34mpg).

Number built: (1966) 1,080,165

Owner: Philip Parmenter

Right: The larger window area of all Beetles built from August 1964-on is **very** evident in this view. The slimmer pillars helped to give a lighter, more airy feel to the interior. This example has been fitted with an accessory trim across the rear louvers and finger-plates under the door handles.

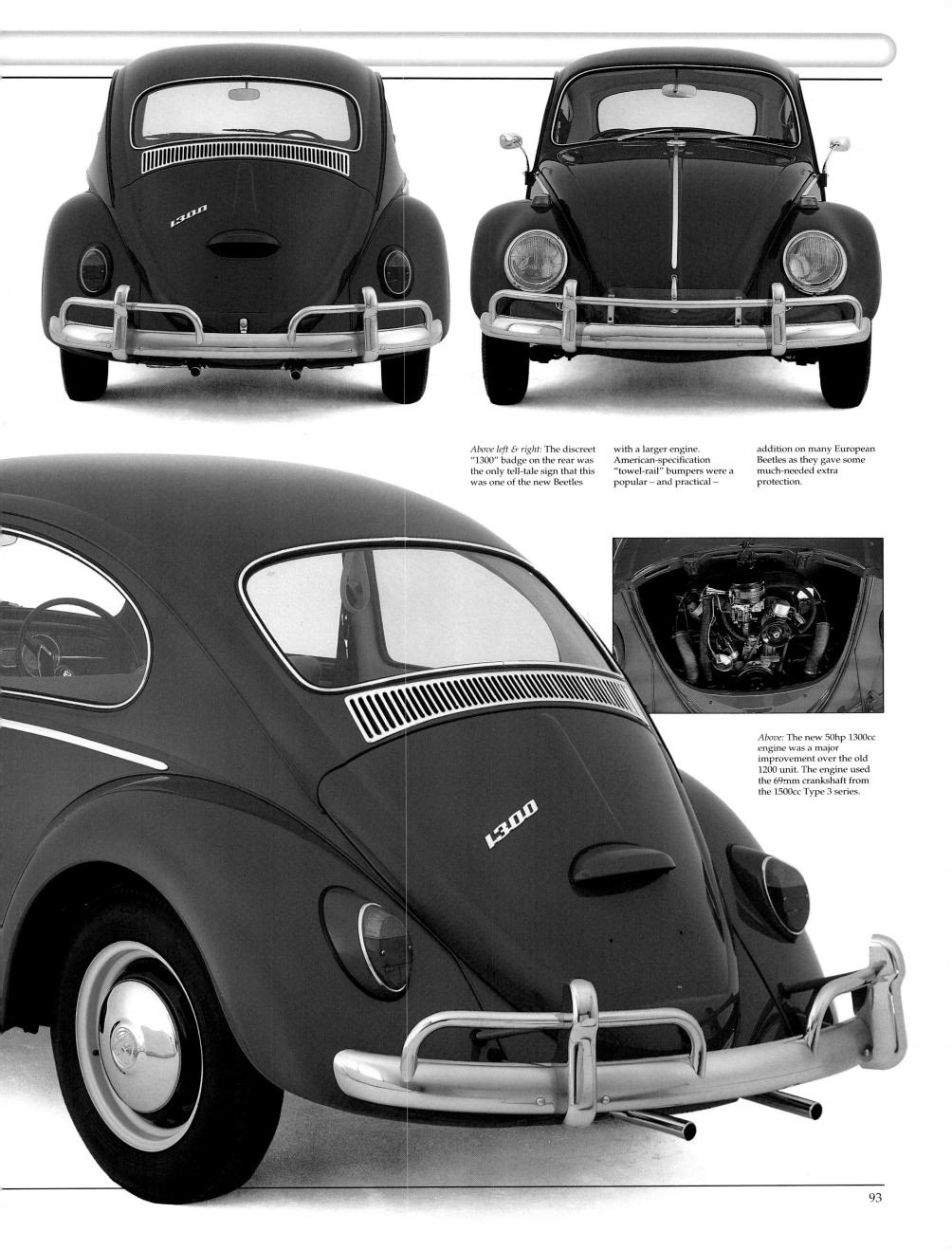

Above left & right: The discreet "1300" badge on the rear was the only tell-tale sign that this was one of the new Beetles with a larger engine. American-specification "towel-rail" bumpers were a popular – and practical – addition on many European Beetles as they gave some much-needed extra protection.

Above: The new 50hp 1300cc engine was a major improvement over the old 1200 unit. The engine used the 69mm crankshaft from the 1500cc Type 3 series.

Of all Beetles built throughout the years, the most sought-after have been the cabriolets. Built by Karmann in Osnabrück, they were based on the regular sedans and, accordingly, shared all the mechanical upgrades. They were the envy of many other manufacturers for the quality of the Karmann conversion was second to none. Indeed, it has often been said that if a passenger was blindfolded, he would be unable to tell if he was traveling in a basic sedan or a cabriolet, for there was little increase in wind-noise and no appreciable loss of rigidity. It is worth noting that the cabriolet would outlast the sedan on the Volkswagen production lines.

Right: The dashboard was identical to that of the sedan. Note the heater vents in the top of the dashboard and down in the passenger footwell. However, heating was still not the Beetle's strong point.

Above: As was the usual case, the engine fitted to the cabriolet was identical to that of the equivalent sedan model, in this case a 50hp 1300 type. Note the current design of air-filter with its pre-heat pipe to supply warm air to the carburetor.

Right: The lines of the cabriolet are best appreciated from the rear three-quarters. To many, the cabriolet models look their best with the top in the raised position. Note the horizontal layout of the louvers in the deck lid, compared with the vertical style of those on the 1956 cabriolet seen earlier.

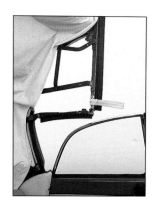

Above: Part of the reason why the Beetle cabriolet was the envy of so many other manufacturers was the complex design of the folding top mechanism.

Above: At the front, the top was secured with these adjustable clamps. The design was so efficient that the cabriolet was as weather-tight as the sedan.

Above right: With the top folded down, the driver's view to the rear was somewhat restricted. A well-fitting top bag was supplied as standard with each cabriolet. Note the chrome frame to each of the side windows.

Right: From the front, the distinctive shape of the cabriolet windshield survived even though the glass area had been increased in August 1964.

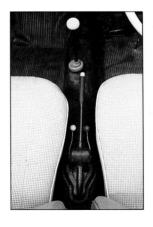

Above: The heater controls were located between the front seats on both sedans and cabriolets. One lever turned the heater on, the other opened the vents under the rear seat.

Left: This design of door handle shows this to be a car built prior to May 1966.

SPECIFICATIONS

Engine: Horizontally opposed, air-cooled four cylinder. Construction: Two-piece cast magnesium-alloy crankcase split vertically with separate cast-iron cylinders and cast aluminum alloy pistons. Four main bearings. Cast aluminum cylinder heads with siamesed inlet ports. **Bore and stroke:** 77mm x 69mm. **Capacity:** 1285cc (78.4ci). **Valves:** Pushrod operated overhead. **Compression ratio:** 7.3:1. **Fuel system:** Mechanical fuel pump; single Solex 28PICT carburetor. **Maximum power:** 40bhp (50 US hp) at 4,000rpm. **Maximum torque:** 70lb ft at 2,000rpm.

Transmission: Fully-synchromesh, four-speed manual transaxle with integral final drive unit. One-piece casing. **Gear ratios:** First – 3.80; second – 2.06; third – 1.32; fourth – 0.89; reverse – 3.88. **Final drive ratio:** 4.375 :1.

Brakes: Hydraulically-operated drums on all four wheels

Steering: Worm and roller

Suspension: Front: Fully independent with transverse, multi-leaf torsion bars and telescopic dampers. Ball-joint design with hydraulic steering damper. **Rear:** Fully independent swing-axle with twin solid torsion bars and telescopic dampers.

Wheels and tires: 4J x 15in pressed steel wheels. 5.60 x 15 cross-ply tires.

Dimensions: Length: 4070mm (13ft 4.2in). **Width:** 1540mm (5ft 0.6in). **Height:** 1500mm (4ft 11in). **Wheelbase:** 2400mm (7ft 10.5in). **Dry weight:** 780kg (1720lb).

Peformance: Maximum speed: 116km/h (72mph). **Acceleration:** 0-96km/h (60mph): c27sec. **Fuel consumption:** 8.1lits/100km (34mpg)

Number built: (1966) 9,712

Owner: Charles Oldroyd

The 1963 Beetles differed little from their predecessor, with the exception of an improved heating system – the new "fresh-air" system was designed to prevent engine fumes from entering the car, while controls under the back seat regulated the flow of warm air to the rear passenger compartment. One small cosmetic detail was the removal of the enameled Wolfsburg crest from the front hood, a sad loss in the eyes of many enthusiasts who saw it as a link with a historic past.

The 1964 Beetle was essentially little different from the 1963 model, with one notable exception: the fabric folding sun-roof, which had been available since 1950, finally made way for a far more sophisticated steel sliding roof on the export models. Standard Beetles, however, retained the fabric roof. The steering wheel was redesigned to incorporate a simple two-thumb horn push which replaced the semi-circular design introduced four years earlier. Other details included larger front turn signals and plain chromed hubcaps – no longer would the VW logo be picked out in black. A total of 1,216, 390 Beetles were built that calendar year, another production record that proved the VW was as popular as ever.

A Clearer View

However, there were big changes afoot for 1965, with the another major redesign of the bodywork taking place in the form of slimmer body pillars and a slightly curved windshield. The effect of these modifications is to make the overall glass area noticeably larger than the old model, with the rear window alone being some 10mm (0.39in) wider and 20mm (0.79in)

Above: In August 1965, the 1300 Beetle was introduced, with a more powerful 1285cc engine which produced 50hp. This "borrowed" the crankshaft from the 1500 engine of the Type 3 range in order to achieve the increased capacity.

Below: An unusual overhead view of the 1966 cabriolet gives a clear indication of the efficient use of space in what is, after all, a small car. The rear-mounted engine and transmission package did not infringe on the passenger space at all.

deeper than before. The windshield was 28mm (1.1in) taller, too. The opening vent wings in the doors changed shape, with their pillars being raked back at a slight angle to give the car a more modern look. At the rear, the familiar T-handle deck lid lock made way for a plain push-button latch which still could not be locked.

More Power

Inside the 1965 model there . were new heater control levers which replaced the old rotary knob which had been used since October 1952. The right-hand lever turned the heating system on while the left-hand one opened or shut the vents under the rear seat. While these changes may have made the Beetle an altogether better car, it was beginning to struggle to stay in the limelight and many dealers must have prayed for something new to tell their customers. Rival manufacturers might not have been able to

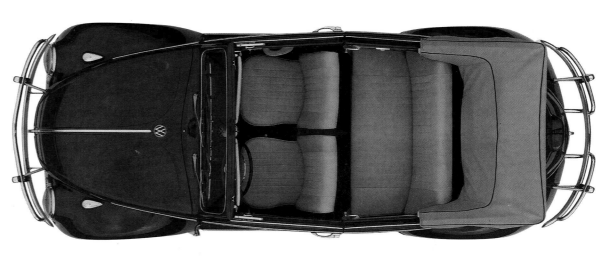

Left: New in 1967 was this redesigned deck lid which concealed another engine option: the 1500. Amazingly, this body style was only offered for one year.

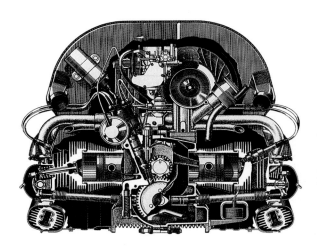

Above: The new 1500 engine was derived from that used in the Type 2 and Type 3 ranges. Generally recognized as being one of the best engines ever offered in the Beetle range, the 53hp unit lasted until 1971, when it was superseded by the 1600 model.

Right: As this picture proves, the Beetle had come a long way since the heady days of 1938. Almost 30 years of development had seen the engine grow from 985cc to 1493cc, and power output from 30hp to 53hp. Even the body styling had noticeably changed.

Right: The most sweeping changes to date were made for the 1968 model year, when a new deck lid, valance, rear lights and bumper design all made their appearance.

Above: The semi-automatic "Stickshift" Beetle only came with two pedals – the clutch was activated when the driver put his hand on the gearshift lever.

Left: The 1968 Beetles also saw upright headlamps fitted across the range – they had first been introduced on the American market one year earlier.

boast of the VW's reliability but they could argue that their cars were more modern, more powerful and more enjoyable to drive. It was difficult not to agree with them, despite the fact that the Beetle's sales figures continued to impress: in the USA, for example, over 295,000 were sold that year. What was needed was more than a cosmetic change if the Beetle was to stay ahead of the competition.

Their prayers were answered when, in August 1965, Volkswagen launched the 1300 Beetle, powered by a 1285cc engine using the 69mm (2.72in) crankshaft from the 1500 Type 3 model. The result was an increase in horsepower from 40hp to 50bhp, a gain of some 25 percent. To distinguish the new model from others, there was a discreet "1300" badge on the deck lid, while a new style of wheel, with ventilation slots around the hubcap, was borrowed from the Type 3 range. A flat hubcap was also fitted, although the familiar domed design remained in use on the 1200cc standard versions.

These 1966 models also featured a re-designed front suspension system, where the original king- and link-pin design was replaced with a more modern ball-joint set-up. At the same time, the number and size of torsion leaves in the front axle beam was changed to improve the ride quality. The result was a car that was far more pleasant to drive and which had a better chance of keeping up with other traffic – the top speed of the 1300 Beetle was a mighty 121km/h (75mph). Although total Beetle production was slightly down at 1,021,298, sales in the vital US market were up by just under 6,000 to 302,423 in 1966.

For 1967, Volkswagen had some big changes in store, all aimed at keeping the

This model saw some of the most significant developments in the Beetle's specification: a new, more powerful engine, front disc brakes (on European models) and revised styling all made the 1967 model year a milestone in Beetle history. In the USA, Volkswagen also added sealed-beam headlamps in redesigned front fenders, as well as updating the electrical system to 12 volts – European versions, however, retained the old-style headlamps and the poor 6-volt system. Visually, the biggest change was the new deck lid, designed to accommodate the larger engine. With more efficient brakes and revised rear suspension, the Beetle was continuing to evolve.

SPECIFICATIONS

Engine: Horizontally opposed, air-cooled four cylinder. **Construction:** Two-piece cast magnesium-alloy crankcase split vertically with separate cast-iron cylinders and cast aluminum alloy pistons. Four main bearings. Cast aluminum cylinder heads with siamesed inlet ports. **Bore and stroke:** 83mm x 64mm. **Capacity:** 1493cc (91ci). **Valves:** Pushrod operated overhead. **Compression ratio:** 7.5:1. **Fuel system:** Mechanical fuel pump; single Solex 30PICT-2 carburetor. **Maximum power:** 44bhp (53 US hp) at 4,000rpm. **Maximum torque:** 78lb ft at 2,600rpm.

Transmission: Fully-synchromesh, four-speed manual transaxle with integral final drive unit. One-piece casing. **Gear ratios:** First – 3.80; second – 2.06; third – 1.26; fourth – 0.89; reverse – 3.88. **Final drive ratio:** 4.125 :1.

Brakes: Hydraulically-operated discs (front) and drums (rear)

Steering: Worm and roller

Suspension: Front: Fully independent with transverse, multi-leaf torsion bars and telescopic dampers. Ball-joint design with hydraulic steering damper. **Rear:** Fully independent swing-axle with twin solid torsion bars, rear stabilizer bar and telescopic dampers.

Wheels and tires: 4J x 15in pressed steel wheels. 5.60 x 15 cross-ply tires.

Dimensions: Length: 4070mm (13ft 4.2in). **Width:** 1540mm (5ft 0.6in). **Height:** 1500mm (4ft 11in). **Wheelbase:** 2400mm (7ft 10.5in). **Dry weight:** 788kg (1737lb).

Peformance: Maximum speed: 135km/h (84mph). **Acceleration:** 0-96km/h (60mph): 22sec. **Fuel consumption:** 7.6lits/100km (32mpg).

Number built: (1967) 925,787

Owner: Paula Riches

Above: The interior light on all models remained located above the left-hand door pillar. Note the plastic headlining.

Above: Although the basic layout of the dashboard remained the same, the switchgear was replaced with new "safety" knobs which were soft to the touch. These were intended to meet the requirements of US safety laws. Little else changed inside the Beetle – it was as austere as ever and long overdue for a redesign.

Right: The most obvious change made for the 1967 model year was the redesigned deck lid, which was now slightly squared-off at the bottom. The trim along the side of the body was also narrower than that used previously. Flat hubcaps concealed new four-bolt wheels on the 1500cc models, these being equipped with disc front brakes – a first for the Beetle. However, 1200 and 1300 models retained the old-style five-bolt wheels and drum brakes.

Above left & right: From the rear, the new deck lid was clearly visible. Its more bulbous design was to allow the fitment of the new 1500 engine introduced in August 1966 and required the provision of a new rear valance. Note, once again, this example has been fitted with American-specification bumpers. At the front, the trim strip on the hood was thinner than before, but that was about all. However, in the USA, Beetles sold in 1967 were fitted with upright, sealed-beam headlamp assemblies, which required new front fenders.

Right: Although the VW logo remained, the Wolfsburg crest had long since disappeared from the bonnet (it was last seen in 1962).

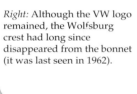

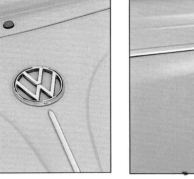

Left: New door locks and handles were fitted in 1967, the latter proving to be a one-year-only feature. The new locks were designed to prevent the door bursting open in an accident. Again, pressure from the US safety lobby brought about this minor change.

Above: The big news for the 1967 model range was the introduction of the 1500cc engine, which had first seen duty in the Type 2 and Type 3 models. In conjunction with improved braking and suspension systems, this engine made the 1500 Beetle one of the best ever.

Right: The turn signals remained unchanged, those at the front being mounted on top of the fenders.

Above: The end of an era came as Heinz Nordhoff was laid to rest, having died on April 12th, 1968. Nordhoff's funeral cortege was lead by a unique Type 2 pick-up on which his coffin was carried through the streets of Wolfsburg. The funeral cars were all Type 3 Notchbacks.

Below: Launched in 1968, the VW 411 was never a success. Too heavy, too slow and too expensive, the Type 4 was a costly mistake.

Right: Carl Hahn had been chosen by Nordhoff as his successor. However, the VW board had other ideas and appointed Kurt Lotz instead.

Beetle at the top of the sales charts. There was a new model introduced in the form of the 1500 Beetle, which used a revised version of the 53hp Type 3 engine and came with disc brakes fitted to the front axle. Well, they were fitted to European models, but the US market inexplicably had to put up with the old drum brakes. For some reason, no Beetle would ever be offered in the USA with disc brakes. However, while the Europeans still had to suffer six-volt electrics, the US-bound VWs were sold with 12-volt systems.

The new 1500 model is generally thought to be the best Beetle ever to be offered, with superior performance, stopping power and handling, thanks to a new "Z-bar," or equalizer spring, incorporated into the rear suspension. American models even came with "upright" sealed-beam headlamps (taken

once again from the Type 3) which greatly improved visibility at night, although European Beetles retained the traditional sloping headlamps for another year. The 1300 Beetle continued to be offered alongside the new model but did not benefit from the improved braking system, while the old 1200 engine was still available in what became known as the 1300A. In January 1967 a new basic Beetle was introduced, called the *Sparkäfer,* or "Economy Beetle." Based on the 1300 model, this bottom-of-the-range Beetle was something of a modern version of the old standard model with basic trim, little chrome and few home comforts. It was intended to help bolster flagging sales.

The 1967 Beetle model range was an expensive exercise for Volkswagen as there were numerous parts that were exclusive to the

model. The deck lid, for example, had to be redesigned to accommodate the new engine, which in turn meant a new rear valance had to be fitted. The door handles, both inside and out, were also unique, being redesigned yet again at the end of the model year. Today, the '67s are sought after by enthusiasts as they represent the best of the "old" style of VW, for 1968 models were, again, very different.

Changes Abound

The most obvious change for '68 was the introduction of heavy "Euro" bumpers designed to meet the more stringent American safety regulations. These clumsy bumpers, while keeping the safety experts happy, did little to enhance the steadily changing appearance of the Beetle. Other improvements made by Wolfsburg included yet another deck lid, this time considerably shorter and more square in design than its predecessor, and an externally-mounted gas filler. New door handles with trigger levers, aimed at preventing the door from bursting open in a roll-over accident, and a collapsible steering column were further safety features. All models now came with the Type 3's upright headlamps, along with a new design of rear light unit on all but the basic Beetle. As far as the running gear was concerned, the old five-bolt style of wheel fitting, in use since the very first KdF-Wagens, finally gave way to a more rigid four-bolt design. But perhaps the biggest improvement of all, on European models, was the introduction of a 12-volt electrical system to bring them in line with their US-specification counterparts.

Perhaps the most technically interesting Beetle to date was introduced this year, the so-

called semi-automatic. This was a 1500 model equipped with a unique three-speed transmission that allowed the driver to change gear without the use of a clutch. In fact, thanks to a torque convertor, the car could be started and driven from rest in any gear. This new model accounted for half of all sales of 1500 Beetles in the first four months of production.

Aside from the transmission, the semi-automatic also featured a far superior rear suspension system, with semi-trailing arms and double-jointed halfshafts. At last Volkswagen appeared to acknowledge that the old swing-axle design had its shortcomings, so much so, in fact, that all Beetles destined for sale in the USA came with the IRS suspension regardless of the type of transmission used. These US-specification models also came with a 1600cc engine. Once again, one has to question why the US market got such preferential treatment when it would have been more cost-effective for the factory to produce the same models for all markets.

End Of An Era

In 1968, Heinz Nordhoff, who had led the Volkswagen organization since the late 1940s, suffered a heart attack and died. Throughout his life at Wolfsburg Nordhoff had been held in high esteem, credited with being the person responsible for ensuring the success of the Beetle. Indeed, Ferdinand Porsche, viewing the production line at Wolfsburg, once turned to Nordhoff and said "You know, Herr Nordhoff, this is the way I always imagined it, but I didn't know I was right until you proved it." There could be no finer epitaph for the man who made Porsche's dream a reality.

Nordhoff had many critics, people who felt the company's reliance on just one model for so long would damage future prospects. Tired of such criticisms, Nordhoff on one occasion gathered together all the design exercises that

Above: The Type 1 Karmann Ghia continued in production from 1955 until its demise in August 1973. In all that time, some 363,401 coupés were built, along with 80,899 cabriolets. The greatest number of these were sold in the USA where the Ghia was well received.

Below: By way of contrast, the Type 3 Karmann Ghia was never such a success. Although its styling was clearly aimed at the US market, the model was never offered for sale in America. Eventually, the Type 3 Ghia was dropped after 42,498 examples had been built.

Left: The Type 4 was an odd mix of styles. In sedan form, as shown, it lacked the rear luggage compartment of the Type 3, despite the compact nature of its engine. Spacious and extremely comfortable, the 411 was a luxurious car which was let down by too many ill-conceived details.

Right: In 1967, the original split-screen Type 2 design was replaced by an all-new model, affectionately called the "bay window" in honor of its panoramic, one-piece windshield. The new model had a higher payload than its predecessor and proved to be a huge success.

For many, this marked the turning point in Volkswagen design. Gone were the smooth, rounded lines of old, replaced instead by more angular styling, with a squared-off deck lid and tail lights, larger, more substantial bumpers and upright headlamps across the range. The changes to the bumpers and lighting were made for safety reasons as the Beetle came under pressure, notably in the USA, from the safety lobby. Other "improvements" included relocating the gas filler to the outside of the car. Some diehard enthusiasts felt that the Beetle had lost its charm while others believed that the changes were made for the better. It is, as they say, all a matter of taste.

SPECIFICATIONS

Engine: Horizontally opposed, air-cooled four cylinder. **Construction:** Two-piece cast magnesium-alloy crankcase split vertically with separate cast-iron cylinders and cast aluminum alloy pistons. Four main bearings. Cast aluminum cylinder heads with siamesed inlet ports. **Bore and stroke:** 77mm x 69mm. **Capacity:** 1285cc (78.4ci). **Valves:** Pushrod operated overhead. **Compression ratio:** 7.3:1. **Fuel system:** Mechanical fuel pump; single Solex 30PICT-2 carburetor. **Maximum power:** 40bhp (50 US hp) at 4,000rpm. **Maximum torque:** 70lb ft at 2,000rpm.

Transmission: Fully-synchromesh, four-speed manual transaxle with integral final drive unit. One-piece casing. **Gear ratios:** First – 3.80; second – 2.06; third – 1.32; fourth – 0.89; reverse – 3.88. **Final drive ratio:** 4.375 :1.

Brakes: Hydraulically-operated drums on all four wheels

Steering: Worm and roller

Suspension: Front: Fully independent with transverse, multi-leaf torsion bars and telescopic dampers. Ball-joint design with hydraulic steering damper. **Rear:** Fully independent swing-axle with twin solid torsion bars, rear stabilizer bar and telescopic dampers.

Wheels and tires: 4J x 15in pressed steel wheels. 5.60 x 15 cross-ply tires.

Dimensions: Length: 4028mm (13ft 2.6in). **Width:** 1540mm (5ft 0.6in). **Height:** 1500mm (4ft 11in). **Wheelbase:** 2400mm (7ft 10.5in). **Dry weight:** 862kg (1900lb).

Peformance: Maximum speed: 127km/h (79mph). **Acceleration:** 0-96km/h (60mph): 22sec. **Fuel consumption:** 8.3lits/100km (34mpg)

Number built: (1968) 1,136,134

Owner: Rob Thatcher

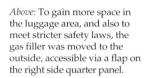

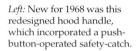

Above: To gain more space in the luggage area, and also to meet stricter safety laws, the gas filler was moved to the outside, accessible via a flap on the right side quarter panel.

Left: New for 1968 was this redesigned hood handle, which incorporated a push-button-operated safety-catch.

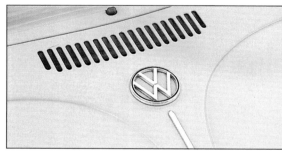

Left: First seen in the USA in 1967, the new upright headlamp design changed the look of the whole front end of the Beetle.

Above: Aware of criticism about a lack of ventilation, the factory finally saw fit to incorporate a fresh-air system.

Left: New door handles, with a trigger release, were intended to prevent the doors opening if the car was rolled on its side in an accident.

Above left & right: There were several major changes to the Beetle's appearance, not the least of which was the fitment of new "Europa" bumpers.

Another new deck lid, shorter and more square than before, replaced that of the 1967 models, while new rear lights also made their first

appearance. Many felt the Beetle had lost its charm, while others felt the changes were for the better. Sales, however, continued to hold steady.

Below: The engines remained the same, although now equipped with 12-volt electrical components on all but the basic 1200 models. VW's philosophy

had long been "if it isn't broken, don't try and fix it." The philosophy had a lot of merit. Note, however, the new valance.

Left: The profile of the Beetle had slowly evolved over the years, the most significant change being the adoption of the new bumpers and upright headlamps. Note also the more bulbous deck lid and the larger rear light clusters.

had been considered throughout the 1950s and early 1960s in an effort to prove that still waters do indeed run deep. However, they could not disguise the fact that Nordhoff's baby, the Type 3, had not been the success he had hoped. There was no getting away from the point that, although the Beetle's days as the number one best seller were numbered, it refused to lie down and die. Indeed, in 1968, American sales reached another all-time high, some 390,000 Beetles being sold in the USA.

New Models?

Nordhoff's successor was Kurt Lotz, who quickly realized that the company had been too successful throughout the 1960s to risk making any sudden changes to the way it was run. However, he did hint at change in the future, with the occasional remark suggesting that new models might be around the corner. One thing that Lotz was well aware of was Volkswagen's heavy dependence on the American market. Following the revaluation of the Deutschmark, Lotz was worried that this would mean a damaging rise in vehicle prices abroad, so he opted to absorb much of the increase, aware of the threat of pressure from other importers – especially those from the Far East. However, some other decisions made while he was in control did the company fewer favors: the Type 4 range was launched in August 1968 and proved to be one of the biggest disappointments in Volkswagen history. Heavy, underpowered and too expensive, the 411 and the later 412, were never the success Lotz had hoped. Had it been launched five years earlier, things might have been different but, as the Americans say, it was a buck too short and a day too late.

However, the last months of the decade were not all doom and gloom, for Volkswagen celebrated the assembly of the 15,000,000th vehicle since the war on November 29th, 1969 and in December announced the formation of a new Swedish import company, Svenska Volkswagen AB, which took over from the old Scania-Vabis concern, which had handled the business since the 1950s.

Looking back over the decade, Volkswagen witnessed some major events in the Beetle's life. First there was the new engine and trans-

Above: Volkswagen established a plant in Brazil as early as 1953. It continued to build Beetles until 1986, at which time production came to a halt. However, it restarted in 1993 when the Brazilian government put pressure on VW to re-introduce the Beetle in their home market.

Right: Volkswagen built Beetles in Australia between 1954 and 1976, assembling them from CKD (Completely Knocked Down) kits shipped from Germany.

Right: Beetles were also assembled at this plant in South Africa between 1951 and 1979, making it one of the longest-lasting satellite factories.

Below: D'Ieteren Frères in Brussels was the official importer into Belgium and assembled Beetles, largely for the home market, between 1954 and 1975.

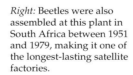

Left: In 1972, VW set up a plant in Indonesia. This was used until 1977, when it was taken over by Daimler-Benz and the Development Aid Corporation.

Above: An impressive line-up of Beetles awaits shipment from Emden to the USA in 1965. Sales were still strong, with some 383,978 Beetles sold in the USA that year.

Right: The Beetle was produced at Emden from 1964 until its eventual demise in sedan form in 1978. This photograph, taken in 1965, shows bodyshells on their way from the paint shop at Emden.

Below right: The first Beetle to leave Emden for the USA. The American market continued to be the most important of all as far as sales were concerned. Volkswagen invested DM 154.4 million in this new assembly plant.

mission, followed by no less than three revised body designs and the introduction of an interesting semi-automatic model. Then, of course, there was the Type 3 range, which included a crisply-styled Karmann Ghia version, a revised Type 2 in 1967 and finally the heavyweight, and ultimately unsuccessful, Type 4. Taking stock of all these developments, it is hard to point a finger at Nordhoff and accuse him of adopting a one-model policy. The Volkswagen range entered the 1970s with a quite staggering variety of vehicles, from the basic 1200 *Sparkäfer* to a four-door, fuel-injected family sedan.

It had become clear, early on in the decade, that the Wolfsburg site would not be able to cope with future production. In view of this, Volkswagen opened a number of factories around the world. There had been an assembly plant in Mexico since 1954 (the current plant was opened in 1967 at Puebla), along with others in Brazil, Belgium, Ireland, South Africa, Australia, New Zealand and the Philippines, all established in the 1950s. In 1961 these were joined by one in Uruguay, then Venezuela in 1963, Portugal in 1964, Peru in 1966 and Malaysia and Singapore in 1968. In addition, there were no fewer than three factories, including Wolfsburg, in Germany: Emden had opened its gates in December 1964 and then, of course, there was Osnabrück, site of the Karmann factory, where Karmann Ghias and Beetle cabriolets continued to be produced and which had started Beetle production in 1949. In addition, Type 2s were built at Hanover.

As a world car, the Volkswagen had arrived, but by now, the name was no longer linked solely with the Beetle.

IMPROVING THE BREED

By the start of the 1970s, it was evident that, if it was to remain as Volkswagen's number one product, the Beetle was in dire need of a redesign. The dilemma here, as far as Volkswagen was concerned, was that any improvements which might make the Beetle a more marketable product would almost certainly be in conflict with the whole *raison d'être* of the model. The Beetle had always sold because it was perceived to be an inexpensive, honest motor car with few frills and no gimmicks. By "improving" the product, the company ran the risk of compromising this honesty which had long been the Beetle's strongest selling point.

However, by now there were fewer diehard Beetle owners – people who would automatically buy a Beetle no matter what other options might be open to them. There was a new generation of customers, who had grown up in the more affluent 1960s, for whom the no-nonsense appeal of the Beetle was not enough to sway their purchasing decisions. If it was inexpensive transport they were seeking, then there were several other companies which offered cheap

Above: Over 30 years after the factory had been founded, Beetle production continued to be its number one priority. However, for VW to maintain its place as number one in Germany, a new model range was called for.

alternatives: the Renault 4, NSU Prinz, even the British Mini.

With the continuing production of the Type 3 models, a steadily revised Type 2 range, the introduction of the unwieldy Type 4 and links with the NSU-Audi empire, Volkswagen had

Right: A marketing man, Rudolph Leiding appeared to be more concerned than his predecessor, Kurt Lotz, about the future of the company and its product range. It was while he was in control that the decision was made to produce the water-cooled Golf and Scirocco.

Below: Leiding inherited a pair of poorly-conceived models: the Type 4 and the disastrous K70. The latter had been designed by NSU and was taken over by Volkswagen so as to broaden the marque's appeal. Technically flawed, the K70 was an expensive failure.

Right: On February 17th, 1972, the Beetle officially became the biggest-selling car of all time (15,007,034 units), taking over the mantle from Ford's legendary Model T.

what was, on the surface, a very impressive line-up. However, the top-selling model was still the Beetle and its fortunes were starting to slip. What was the answer? According to Kurt Lotz and his successor – in October 1971 – Rudolph Leiding, the solution was a "new" Beetle. Perhaps it would also be fair to say, a new water-cooled car as well: the K70.

The K70 was a disaster for Volkswagen. Conceived as an NSU and inherited by Volkswagen when it acquired the Neckarsülm company in 1969, the K70 was something new as far as VW was concerned. The angular three-box sedan was powered by an in-line, front-mounted water-cooled engine which drove the front wheels via a transaxle unit. Loosely based on the old NSU air-cooled engine, the K70's powerplant produced 100bhp from its 1700cc. Several pundits at the time questioned the wisdom of Volkswagen marketing a car which was so close in size and price to the existing Type 4 models, but VW ignored such comments. In hindsight it is easy to suggest that instead of one millstone round its neck, Wolfsburg now had two to contend with…

A Costly Error?

The K70 proved to be an expensive and unwise diversion as far as Volkswagen's long term future was concerned. The car was never a success despite massive pre-launch publicity and a sales drive which proclaimed it as the way ahead in automotive design. The appalling aerodynamics (a Cd figure of 0.51 – the Beetle's was only 0.44!) resulted in poor fuel economy, while it cost so much to build that it could never be a profitable model for the company. Indeed, as a whole, Volks-

Below: New for 1971 was a revised engine range, with 1300 and 1600 versions being offered in the majority of markets. The 1200 continued to be available in base-model vehicles.

Above: The revised engines were equipped with all-new cylinder heads which featured dual inlet ports. However, the earlier single-port design continued on the smaller 1200 engine. Apart from some fairly minor revisions, this design continued in use into the 1990s in South America.

wagen's profits fell by over 40 percent at this time and Kurt Lotz was considered to be largely to blame for this down-turn in the company's fortunes, although it has to be said that this was a period when there was considerable financial upheaval in Western Europe as a whole.

With few changes to the Beetle for the 1970 model year, many potential customers delayed buying a new car in the hope that the new year would see some sign of change. Many Europeans felt disappointed that they had been denied the introduction of the IRS (independent rear suspension) system enjoyed by the Americans since 1968. True, it did seem illogical to build one car for the USA and another for the domestic market, but VW appeared adamant initially that there was no

need to introduce the new suspension design closer to home.

Despite offering a variety of engine and model combinations, such as a 1200 with the 1300 engine, or a 1300 with a 1200 engine as well as the 1500, with either manual or semi-automatic transmission, Wolfsburg's 1970 line-up looked little different to previous models. However, 1971 was to change all that.

Introduced to the world as the Super Beetle, the 1302 and 1302S models were heralded as being the ultimate development of the People's Car. The former was powered by a development of the old 1300 engine, now equipped with all-new dual-port cylinder heads with separate inlet ports for each cylinder (all previous cylinder heads used a single siamesed inlet port) which produced 53hp, while the latter came with a new 1600cc engine producing 57hp. To help overcome the long-term problem of the oil cooler blocking the cooling airflow to number three cylinder (this was always the most likely to seize), the engine shrouding was redesigned and the oil cooler was now mounted externally and fed by extra ductwork.

New Suspension

The new engine was a revelation and remains one of the best ever fitted to the Beetle. It was not only more powerful and more torquey, but also – in theory at least – more reliable, with a redesigned crankcase and improved oil system. However, the most interesting aspect of the new models could be found underneath that familiar bodywork: not only was the US-only IRS suspension system finally made available to Europeans, but there was an all-new front suspension design, too. Forsaking Ferdinand Porsche's beloved torsion bar design, which had been in use since the very first prototypes built before World War II, Volkswagen engineers adopted an advanced MacPherson strut front suspension system which considerably changed the whole handling characteristics of the Beetle. The system was similar to that which had been used on the Type 4 range since its introduction three years earlier.

The new front suspension also allowed the designers to increase the luggage carrying capacity, as the trunk could be made deeper

Left: The dual-port engines also included a revised oil-cooling system which placed the cooling radiator outside the fan-housing for improved air-flow over number 3 cylinder. This was designed to help prevent costly engine failures.

Below: The new 1302 range, launched for the 1971 model year, featured a radically different front suspension system: the MacPherson strut. First seen on the Type 4 in 1968, the new design allowed better use to be made of the front luggage area.

Left: The 1302 certainly appeared to be more practical, with its increased luggage capacity, but the revised styling did little to broaden the Beetle's appeal. The model lasted just two years before being replaced by the 1303 range.

and wider, with the spare wheel now being laid down flat in front of a relocated gas tank. The result was a massive increase in volume, from just under $0.14m^3$ (5cu ft) to a little over $0.25m^3$ (9cu ft). Add this to the space that had always been available behind the rear seat and, over 30 years after it was designed, the Beetle suddenly became a true family car with a worthwhile carrying capacity.

While the new engine and suspension specification may have brought a smile to the face of many potential customers, the revised styling did little to endear the 1302 and 1302S models to the dyed-in-the-wool enthusiast. Taking advantage of the new front suspension, the stylists saw fit to make the nose of the new models somewhat fatter, more bulbous and hence more capacious than their predecessors. However, the redesign, although subtle as far as the casual observer was concerned, required not only new inner fenders to accommodate the MacPherson strut suspension, but also a new spare-wheel well, gas tank mounting panel, fenders, hood and front valance. Other areas of the bodyshell were revised, with a new through-flow ventilation system, with vents let into the rear quarter panels behind the rear side windows, and a redesigned engine cover adding to the new look. The floorpan was all-new, too, making this by far the most extensive – and costly – revision of the Beetle to be undertaken since it was first launched.

No 1 In America

With hindsight, it is questionable whether the expenditure was worth it for, with the introduction of the K70, the writing appeared to be on the wall for the air-cooled Volks-

Above: During the 1970s, the basic 1200 Beetle continued to offer inexpensive, no-frills motoring. With little in the way of trim, the 1200A was probably more faithful to the original ideals than any other late-model VW.

Right: Breaking the world record and becoming the most successful car of all time was, indeed, cause for celebration. Rudolph Leiding addresses his work-force at Wolfsburg.

Below: Ford disputed VW's claims shortly after, having discovered new evidence of further Model T production. However, the Beetle continued in production and soon there could be no argument about the right to wear the *Weltmeister* crown.

wagen. Or was it? Certainly sales in the USA continued a downward trend from 366,790 in 1970 to 331,191 in 1971 and there were no signs of a U-turn. However, the Beetle remained the number one imported car in North America. In spite of the down-turn in sales, the factory continued to develop the Beetle still further, as well as offering the basic 1200 and 1300 Beetles in Europe with their torsion bar front suspension and swing-axle rear end.

Another New Face

In October 1971, Kurt Lotz stepped down as head of Volkswagen, to be replaced by Rudolph Leiding, who had cut his teeth with Volkswagen back in the early Nordhoff days, acting as deputy in the service department until 1958, when he was put in charge of the Kassel plant, which assembled transmissions. After a spell with the ailing Auto-Union company, Leiding was then appointed head of VW do Brazil, the South American manufacturing facility that had been set up by Nordhoff's longtime ally, Friedrich Schultz-Wenk. He eventually arrived at Wolfsburg at a time when some serious rethinking was necessary, not only as far as the Beetle was concerned, but for the range as a whole.

The new-look Beetle remained fairly much unchanged for 1972. The rear window was enlarged by 40mm (1.57in), top to bottom, while the through-flow ventilation vents were modified to prevent water from getting into the car while stationary. The engine lid was redesigned with four sets of vents, in place of two and, as a consequence, the drainage tray,

which had been fitted to prevent rain from entering the engine compartment, was deleted. To prevent any problems with water soaking the electrical system, Volkswagen improved the damp-proofing of the distributor and coil.

There were other less obvious changes made, too. For example, the door-handle trigger releases were made longer, necessitating a modification to the door panel itself. Bumper mountings were altered, the steering wheel and switchgear redesigned, the body mount-

ings were changed slightly, the lock on the deck lid modified – all were considered necessary by the Volkswagen engineers, but one has to question, yet again, the wisdom of such minor redesigning when they must have realized there was yet another "new" Beetle on the way.

The greatest news of all for Volkswagen in 1972 was that on February 17th, the Beetle finally became the biggest selling car of all time, with sales totalling 15,007,034. VW marked this occasion with the launch of a

special Marathon edition. This took the title away from the Ford Model T, the remarkable vehicle which had been a source of inspiration to both Ferdinand Porsche and Adolf Hitler so many years before. Another milestone was passed in October when the 3,000,000th exchange engine was produced by the Kassel plant. The old and overweight 411 range was phased out, making way for the sharper-looking 412 models, but they did not match up to Volkswagen's sales department's expectations either.

A Whole New Look

The new 1973 model year saw the ever-changing face of the Beetle undergo yet further alteration, by far the biggest ever. The result was the 1303 range which, unlike any previous Beetles, came with a deep, panoramic, curved windshield. This major change of direction was partly to allow more interior space for the front seat passengers as

Left: Wolfsburg's marketing department came up with a seemingly endless variety of special models, each of which was designed to create more interest in the aging Beetle. The oddly-named "1303 Big" (left and center) and the Jeans model did little to improve the Beetle's flagging sales.

Below left: The Yellow and Black Racer was launched at a time when most people were thinking about economy, not performance. Now a sought-after model, it was not the answer.

Above: The denim interior of the Jeans Beetle may have looked attractive when new, but it soon became worn and made the car look untidy. Most Jeans Beetles have since had the seats replaced.

Below: The Jeans Beetle remains one of the more successful special editions, being available in several markets. Note the sports wheels fitted to this example, compared to the plain black hubcaps seen in the photograph to the left.

Although there had been significant styling changes made in 1967 and 1968, the introduction of first the 1302 in 1971 and then the 1303 in 1973 meant that the appearance of the Beetle would never be the same again – or would it? With their wide, bulbous noses to accommodate the new MacPherson strut front suspension, which allowed much more luggage to be carried, the new Beetles looked quite different to their forebears. Redesigned rear suspension resulted in a better ride and improved handling characteristics, too. The 1303 model, seen here, came with a large, panoramic windshield which resulted in more interior space and improved aerodynamics.

SPECIFICATIONS

Engine: Horizontally opposed, air-cooled four cylinder. **Construction:** Two-piece cast magnesium-alloy crankcase split vertically with separate cast-iron cylinders and cast aluminum alloy pistons. Four main bearings. Cast aluminum cylinder heads with separate inlet ports. **Bore and stroke:** 85.5mm x 69mm. **Capacity:** 1584cc (96.6ci). **Valves:** Pushrod operated overhead. **Compression ratio:** 7.5:1. **Fuel system:** Mechanical fuel pump; single Solex 34PICT-3 carburetor. **Maximum power:** 50bhp (53 US hp) at 4,000rpm. **Maximum torque:** 72lb ft at 2,800rpm.

Transmission: Fully-synchromesh, four-speed manual transaxle with integral final drive unit. One-piece casing. **Gear ratios:** First – 3.78; second – 2.06; third – 1.32; fourth – 0.89; reverse – 3.79. **Final drive ratio:** 4.125 :1.

Brakes: Hydraulically-operated discs (front), drums (rear)

Steering: Worm and roller

Suspension: Front: Fully independent with MacPherson strut coil springs and dampers. Steering damper. Rear: Fully independent four-jointed with twin solid torsion bars, rear stabilizer bar and telescopic dampers.

Wheels and tires: 4.5J x 15in pressed steel wheels. 6.00 x 15 cross-ply tires.

Dimensions: Length: 4150mm (13ft 7.4in). Width: 1549mm (5ft 1in). Height: 1501mm (4ft 11in). Wheelbase: 2400mm (7ft 10.5in). Dry weight: 870kg (1918lb).

Performance: Maximum speed: 135km/h (84mph). Acceleration: 0-96km/h (60mph): 18.4sec. Fuel consumption: 8.3lits/100km (34mpg)

Number built: (1968) 791,053

Owner: Peter Spragg

Below: First seen in the 1971 1302S models, the 1600cc engine was one of the finest, although prone to valve and piston problems if not maintained correctly. This engine featured dual-inlet port cylinder heads. Note the alternator.

Right: The handbrake lever and heater controls remained conventionally located between the seats.

Above: Inside the 1303 models, the single biggest change was the new dashboard, with its extensive padding and relocated instrumentation. A new steering wheel was also fitted – both these major changes were made with safety in mind.

Left: Sports wheels of this type were a popular fitment on Beetles of this era. They were available with either 4.5J or 5.5J rims.

Right: The 1303 models were unique in that they came with a new, curved, panoramic windshield. This improved the aerodynamics considerably, but at the expense of some of the

Beetle's long-held character. Also evident in this profile view is the bulbous nose and reshaped front fenders.

Above left & right: At first glance, there appears to be little different about the 1303 models when viewed head-on or from the back, but note the wider, more rounded front end and the larger rear light assemblies. Note also the extra air intake louvers stamped into the deck lid, rather like those of the cabriolet models.

Above: By using MacPherson strut front suspension, the luggage area could be considerably enlarged. Note the upper suspension mountings at each side.

Above: Large rear light cluster earned the nickname "elephant's feet", and not without reason. Fitted to comply with American safety requirements, they made the Beetle far more visible in poor weather conditions.

the dashboard could now be mounted further away. The traditional plain metal dashboard made way for one with plenty of padding, giving greater protection for the occupants of the car in the event of an accident. The instruments were now housed in a separate binnacle directly in front of the driver, while a totally revised ventilation and demisting system helped keep the passengers cool in summer and the windscreen clear in winter.

Further Changes

In addition to the radical restyling of the windshield and scuttle panel, the roof was made less curved and the rear fenders redesigned. These were changed to accommodate all-new rear light assemblies which were soon nick-named "elephants' feet" because of their large, round shape. For many purists, this extensive revamp of Ferdinand Porsche's brain-child was one step too far and there are many who consider the 1303 models to be the

Left: New cars left Wolfsburg by rail, using a station constructed alongside the factory. In the distant background can be seen Schloss Wolfsburg keeping watch over the new cars.

Above: Launched in May 1974, the new water-cooled, front-wheel drive Golf effectively put the nail in the coffin of Beetle production at Wolfsburg. It would go on to be a world beater, too.

least attractive Beetles of all. However, those with a less blinkered outlook can rightly claim that the 1303 range – particularly the 1600cc 1303S – was the best that Volkswagen had ever offered with the most powerful engines, the most sophisticated suspension, the most interior space, the best heating and ventilation system, disc brakes, excellent luggage capacity and a good build quality. But was it still a Beetle? After all, wasn't the Beetle supposed to be a basic means of transport for the masses?

Left: The Beetle's days at Wolfsburg were numbered and production finally came to an end there at 11.19am on July 1st, 1974. However, the streets of the town continued to be crowded with Volkswagens, while the four famous chimneys appeared to look down with fatherly approval.

During 1973, there were several revisions made to the model range, including the Economy Beetle (the old *Sparkäfer*) which was now fitted with the large new rear lights from the 1303 model and black-painted Euro bumpers. There was a 1200L model which, as the title suggests, was a de luxe version of the basic flat-screen Beetle with chromed bumpers, better interior trim, reversing lights and a choice of either the 40hp 1200 or 53hp 1300 engines. Both the 1303 and 1303S could be ordered with the "L" specification, offering a higher standard of trim throughout, but there was also a 1303A for the home market which was a low-spec Super Beetle with the 1200 engine.

Special Models

This was an era when Volkswagen tried various marketing tactics in an effort to rekindle interest in the Beetle ahead of the launch of the new water-cooled range the following year. First there was the Yellow and Black Racer model which was nothing more than a 1303S with yellow bodywork, black hood and deck lid, 5.5J x 15 sports wheels with 175/70 tires and black bumpers. Later the same year, in preparation for the 1974 season, Volkswagen announced the Big Beetle which was a 1303S with the same sports wheel and tire combination, black stripes along the bottoms of the doors and a "1303 Big" decal.

Then there was the crazy, but immensely popular, Jeans Beetle which was a basic 1200 in deep yellow with a denim interior designed to look like a pair of Levi's jeans. Blacked-out body trim and bumpers helped keep the cost to a minimum. The Jeans model, although nothing more than an inexpensive marketing exercise, has proved to be one of the most enduring of all late-model Beetles. Original

Above: Tony Schmücker took over from Rudolph Leiding in 1975 and embarked upon a period of streamlining the work-force. This was necessary to reduce costs as VW now had debts of an estimated DM800 million.

Right: The basic Beetle became even more basic in the 1970s, with plastic caps instead of proper hubcaps, black-painted bumpers and minimal interior trim.

Left: Cabriolet models continued to be popular, especially in America where sales remained steady. Production continued at the Karmann factory in Osnabrück up until 1980.

versions are quite sought after, as the denim upholstery material wore badly in daily use and was often replaced with the regular black vinyl trim.

There were few major changes to the specification of 1974 models compared with that of the previous year's. For the USA, the bumper mountings were changed to a shock-absorbing design, to keep abreast of the latest safety regulations which required that a car should be able to withstand an 8km/h (5mph) impact without sustaining damage. There were also a number of minor improvements made to the engine, including twin pre-heat pipes on the inlet manifold, modified carburetor, a redesigned exhaust system and new heat exchangers, but that was all. However, there were other changes afoot and an important new arrival on the scene.

Water-Cooled Cousins

In March 1974, the Volkswagen Scirocco was launched, followed closely by the Golf in May. The latter was a small family hatchback, powered by a transversely-mounted, four-cylinder, water-cooled engine driving the front wheels. A far cry from the poorly conceived K70, the Golf and its more sporting Scirocco stable-mate soon earned favorable reviews from the motoring press. Many even went so far as to suggest that this was indeed the end of the road for the Beetle. After all, the Golf offered superior performance, greater interior space and superior luggage-carrying capacity. It was faster, more fuel-efficient and no more expensive to buy.

The saddest news of all in 1974 was the announcement that on July 1st the very last Beetle would roll off the assembly line at

Above: Henry Ford's immortal line "You can have it any color you like, so long as it's black" never did apply to the Beetle. By the mid-1970s, a wide variety of colors were available, although blue and red appeared to be the most popular.

Left: In an effort to meet the strict anti-emissions regulations in the USA, a fuel-injection system was fitted to all Beetles destined for the American market. Complex and occasionally unreliable, the system was not popular with owners.

Right: In line with the cabriolet's slightly more up-market image, the factory offered a range of accessories to allow the owner to personalize his car. Note the ATS alloy wheels and extra driving lamps fitted to this example.

Wolfsburg, but the good news was that production would continue at the Emden plant where all US-specification Beetles had been built since the end of 1964, although the bodyshells continued to be produced at Wolfsburg. Since the end of the war, a total of 11,916,519 Beetles had been built at the original Volkswagen factory.

For 1975, there were changes afoot at Wolfsburg, for Rudolph Leiding resigned his chairmanship of Volkswagen AG on January 10th. One month later, Tony Schmücker, a member of the company's advisory committee, was appointed chairman. The Beetle range was now reduced considerably, as the factory acknowledged the shift in demand in the marketplace. Most of the changes seen this year were made were for reasons of economy, such as fitting small plastic dust caps instead of real metal hubcaps on the 1200 models. There was no glovebox lid, either. The front turn signals were now incorporated into the front bumpers across the range, placing them where they are at their most vulnerable to parking damage. The 1303 range – now simply badged as "1303" regardless of engine size or trim specification – did, however, benefit from the fitting of a rack-and-pinion steering system in place of the old steering box.

Fuel-Injection

The big news on the American market was the introduction of fuel-injection on the Beetle engine in an effort to meet the ever-more stringent exhaust emission regulations. The system, manufactured by Robert Bosch, was a relatively simple design, with a fuel loop ("ring main") which supplied the injector units with fuel at a constant pressure. The

Above: In 1974, Beetle production ceased at Wolfsburg, its home since before the war. Now it was down to the workers at Emden to keep the production lines going.

Right: Although some people believe the earlier models to be better built than later examples, Volkswagen always ensured that each and every Beetle was the subject of meticulous scrutiny by a team of highly-skilled inspectors.

Left: In 1975, Volkswagen founded a new assembly plant in Nigeria. It was only a matter of time before there was cause for celebration, this time to mark the completion of the 1,000th Nigerian-built Beetle.

Above: The Nigerian plant at Lagos assembled Beetles in CKD form from kits supplied by Emden and, later, Brazil. The locally-sourced work-force, of just 1,100 people, helped to produce a planned 60 Beetles every day, a far cry from the heyday of Wolfsburg in the 1960s. Incidentally, alongside the Beetle, the Lagos plant also assembled Volkswagen Passat and Audi 100 models for the domestic market.

The mid-1970s saw a change in approach towards the Beetle, with the techically more complex 1302 and 1303 Super Beetles being dropped after just four years of production. A return was made to a more basic specification, with the trustworthy 1192cc engine and swing-axle transmission once again forming the backbone of Beetle production. The examples built during the mid-1970s were often an amalgamation of styles, with this 1975 Type 1 being a perfect example: the rear lights are those first seen on the 1303 range, while the remainder of the bodywork is virtually identical to that of the 1968 Beetles. Time was starting to run out.

SPECIFICATIONS

Engine: Horizontally opposed, air-cooled four cylinder. **Construction:** Two-piece cast magnesium-alloy crankcase split vertically with separate cast-iron cylinders and cast aluminum alloy pistons. Four main bearings. Cast aluminum cylinder heads with siamesed inlet ports. **Bore and stroke:** 77mm x 69mm. **Capacity:** 1192cc (72ci). **Valves:** Pushrod operated overhead. **Compression ratio:** 7.0:1. **Fuel system:** Mechanical fuel pump; single Solex 30PICT-2 carburetor. **Maximum power:** 34bhp (40 US hp) at 3,600rpm. **Maximum torque:** 61lb ft at 2,000rpm.

Transmission: Fully-synchromesh, four-speed manual transaxle with integral final drive unit. One-piece casing. **Gear ratios:** First – 3.80; second – 2.06; third – 1.32; fourth – 0.89; reverse – 3.88. **Final drive ratio:** 4.375 :1.

Brakes: Hydraulically-operated drums on all four wheels

Steering: Worm and roller

Suspension: Front: Fully independent with transverse, multi-leaf torsion bars and telescopic dampers. Ball-joint design with hydraulic steering damper. Rear: Fully independent swing-axle with twin solid torsion bars, rear stabilizer bar and telescopic dampers.

Wheels and tires: 4J x 15in pressed steel wheels. 5.60 x 15 cross-ply tires.

Dimensions: Length: 4028mm (13ft 2.6in). Width: 1540mm (5ft 0.6in). Height: 1500mm (4ft 11in). Wheelbase: 2400mm (7ft 10.5in). Dry weight: 862kg (1900lb).

Peformance: Maximum speed: 127km/h (79mph). Acceleration: 0-96km/h (60mph): 22sec. Fuel consumption: 8.3lits/100km (34mpg).

Number built: (1975) 441,116

Owner: John Burt

Right: The interior was in stark contrast to that of the 1303 model, the dashboard retaining the appearance of the earlier 1200 models. Note the total lack of embellishment and the plain, black steering wheel.

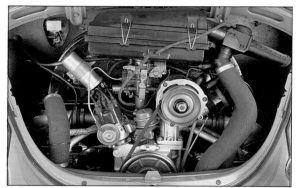

Left: The trusty 40hp, 1192cc engine, first seen in August 1960, still soldiered on, having outlived its more powerful counterparts.

Above: The front hood handle remained unchanged with the exception of a black release button. Note white plastic sealing gasket between handle and bodywork.

Left: The front turn signals were moved from the tops of the fenders to a somewhat vulnerable new location in the front bumper.

Right: With the introduction of the basic model, the Beetle regained much of its earlier character – gone were the "modern" curved windshield and bulbous nose; in their place was the traditional "flat" windshield and 1968-style front end. Note the air vents behind the rear side windows.

Above left & right: From the rear, the styling had become very plain once again, with no badging or other trim.

Note the larger rear window area, first seen in August 1971. From the front, the appearance was very much the same as that of the 1968 models. Sealed-beam headlamps were a major improvement.

Right: The luggage area was virtually identical to that of the pre-1302 and 1303 models. The spare wheel was, once again, located in an upright position ahead of the front axle beam. Note the windshield washer bottle is pressurized from the spare tire. This often led to the tire losing air pressure.

Right: Plain interior trim was exemplified by the door panel, which had simple black handles and only a map pocket as a token gesture towards refinement.

injectors were triggered by a second set of contact points in the distributor. The system worked well but did little to improve either the performance or the fuel economy of the Beetle. Models with this Bosch system installed could be identified by the single exhaust tailpipe and the "Fuel Injection" badge on the deck lid. To accommodate the redesigned exhaust system, a new rear valance was fitted – this appeared on all models, regardless of whether an injection engine was fitted or not.

Back To Basics

For the Beetle, this was almost the end of the road as far as further development was concerned. On July 31st, 1975, the last 1303s came off the production line at Emden, to leave just the basic 1200 models to keep the Beetle going in sedan form. Even the 1300 engine option was dropped from the line-up. The curved windscreen did, however, continue to be a

Left: The Triple White cabriolet was another marketing exercise on the part of Volkswagen to promote sales in the USA. The all-white interior looked attractive but was not the most practical choice for everyday use.

Below: The combination of white bodywork and a white top was certainly eye-catching. Whitewall tires were a standard fitment on certain cabriolets for the US market only.

feature of the cabriolet models which were still being built at Osnabrück by Karmann. Most of these were destined to cross the Atlantic, where sales of convertible cars remained steady.

In Europe, the customer could only buy a Beetle with swing-axle rear suspension, torsion bar front and a 1200 engine, although a 1600 could be supplied to order. The Beetle now seemed very much down the list of Volkswagen's priorities, on home territory at least. Abroad, a new factory in Lagos, Nigeria, opened in March 1975 to assemble Beetles at the rate of 60 each day. In Mexico, 550 cars a day were built at the Puebla factory.

Sales in America showed a marked downward trend in 1975, not so much due to any loss of interest in the product, but because the factory dramatically cut back production. In fact, a total of only 267,815 Beetles were built in calendar year 1975, as opposed to 818,456 the previous year. Of these, just 82,030 were sold in the USA as opposed to 344,177 in 1972, 350,357 in 1973 and 226,098 in 1974. To try and appeal to the public, a special edition "La Grande Bug" was sold in the USA in the 1975 model year, the demand for which was so great that a second and third series had to be built. However, for the first time ever, Volkswagen lost the title of number one exporter to the USA, that claim now being made by the Japanese.

There were no changes made for 1976, except that it was no longer possible to buy a Beetle with a six-volt electrical system. Yes, until August 1976, the basic model Beetle was still available in some markets with the old style electrical system! By this time, even the simple matter of buying a spare headlamp bulb would have been a problem in some places, let alone trying to find a new radio for

Above: Production continued at Emden for a further four years after it ceased at Wolfsburg. However, the end was in sight for the German-built Beetle.

your basic Beetle. Apart from this revelation, there were two other landmarks to give cause for celebration at Wolfsburg: the 1,000,000th Golf and the 30,000,000th Volkswagen were produced in 1976. The year's total Beetle production was just 176,287, of which only 26,794 found their way to the USA. The writing was on the wall for the world's best-selling car, despite the introduction on the US market of the attractive "Triple White" special edition cabriolet with its white paintwork, white top and white interior trim.

There were to be few changes made in 1977 and it was announced in the USA that this was the last year that a sedan model would be available. The decision caused much sadness among Volkswagen fans in America, although they could console themselves with the fact that they could still buy a cabriolet. With just 101,292 Beetles built to satisfy the whole world, it is not surprising that American sales dropped still further to 19,245 that year.

End Of The Line

On January 19th, 1978, the last Beetle sedan to be built on German soil left the assembly line at Emden, although the cabriolet continued to be built at the Karmann coachworks, still in 1303 curved windshield format. Instead, all future Beetles would be imported into Germany from the Mexico factory and

Left: On January 19th, 1978, the very last Beetle sedan to be built on German soil left the production line at Emden.

Above: Production of the cabriolet continued at Osnabrück. The Champagne model was built for the USA.

The unthinkable happened in 1978 when, on January 19th, the very last Beetle sedan to be built on German soil rolled off the line at Emden. This marked the end of an era which had begun almost 40 years earlier when the original VW38 prototypes gained the approval of the world's motoring press. These last German sedans were often supplied in Metallic Diamond Silver, like this example which has less than 1,000km (600 miles) on the odometer. In many ways, these last-of-the-line Beetles shared more with their earliest forebears than any other: they were basically equipped, mechanically simple and offered reasonable – but not exceptional – value for money.

Above: The 1192cc engine remained unaltered – there was very little point in making any major changes as the end of the line was in sight. Note the substantial air-filter assembly used on late-model Beetles.

Left: The front luggage area was identical to that of previous models. Note the rubber trim fitted to the bumpers.

Above: The dashboard retained the black plastic safety padding first introduced on the American market in 1968. The steering wheel was again similar in style to that fitted to the 1303 models and the early water-cooled VWs. The wheel and the padding were weak attempts at updating a rapidly aging design.

Above: The rear licence plate light housing was now made of plastic and featured styling ribs in the top surface. Note lack of louvers in the engine lid – these last of the line German-built Beetles were very basic.

SPECIFICATIONS

Engine: Horizontally opposed, air-cooled four cylinder. **Construction:** Two-piece cast magnesium-alloy crankcase split vertically with separate cast-iron cylinders and cast aluminum alloy pistons. Four main bearings. Cast aluminum cylinder heads with siamesed inlet ports. **Bore and stroke:** 77mm x 69mm. **Capacity:** 1192cc (72ci). **Valves:** Pushrod operated overhead. **Compression ratio:** 7.0:1. **Fuel system:** Mechanical fuel pump; single Solex 30PICT carburetor. **Maximum power:** 34bhp (40 US hp) at 3,600rpm. **Maximum torque:** 61lb ft at 2,000rpm.

Transmission: Fully-synchromesh, four-speed manual transaxle with integral final drive unit. One-piece casing. **Gear ratios:** First – 3.80; second – 2.06; third – 1.32; fourth – 0.89; reverse – 3.88. **Final drive ratio:** 4.375 :1.

Brakes: Hydraulically-operated drums on all four wheels

Steering: Worm and roller

Suspension: Front: Fully independent with transverse, multi-leaf torsion bars and telescopic dampers. Ball-joint design with hydraulic steering damper. **Rear:** Fully independent swing-axle with twin solid torsion bars, rear stabilizer bar and telescopic dampers.

Wheels and tires: 4J x 15in pressed steel wheels. 5.60 x 15 cross-ply tires.

Dimensions: Length: 4028mm (13ft 2.6in). **Width:** 1540mm (5ft 0.6in). **Height:** 1500mm (4ft 11in). **Wheelbase:** 2400mm (7ft 10.5in). **Dry weight:** 862kg (1900lb).

Peformance: Maximum speed: 127km/h (79mph). **Acceleration:** 0-96km/h (60mph): 22sec. **Fuel consumption:** 8.3lits/100km (34mpg)

Number built: (1978) 271,673

Owner: John Lamb

Above: Cord material was used for seating, giving the interior a slightly more luxurious feel. Heater controls and handbrake were in the usual location. Note the black gearshift lever and knob.

Left: This door-mounted mirror was first seen in 1968 and remained in use to the end. Only one mirror was fitted to the driver's side.

Above left& right: The metallic silver paintwork was typical of the last of the German-built cars and suited the lines of the Beetle well. However, the paint earned a reputation for not being very weather resistant.

Right: Blue trim almost looks out of place in a Beetle, but contrasts well with the silver paintwork. The vent wing was an open invitation to car thieves.

Left: This, then, marks the end of the road for the Beetle sedan in Germany – it was no longer built at Wolfsburg, coming instead from Emden. The story of the Beetle in Europe was almost at a close.

built to the current Mexican specification. This included the trusty 40hp 1200 engine, torsion bar front suspension, swing-axle rear, flat windshield and a smaller rear window like those used on German models between 1965 and 1971. At least the "old" window now featured a heating element. The Mexican Beetles appeared to be less austere than the last of the European-produced cars, with chrome hubcaps and trim, radial tires, inertia reel seat belts, anti-dazzle mirror and adjustable head restraints. However, there was no longer the option of the more powerful 57hp 1600 engine.

Swan Song

In the USA, the second of a series of special "Champagne" models was launched. These were first sold in 1977 to celebrate, of all things, the sale of 1,000,000 Golfs, or Rabbits as they were known in the USA. While this was a milestone that probably held little interest as far as the Beetle owner was concerned, the resultant special edition cabriolet was much sought after at the time and remains so to this day. The specification included special paintwork in Red Metallic or Ancona Blue Metallic, an ivory-colored top and interior trim, wood-paneled dashboard, quartz clock, whitewall tires and sports

Above: The Beetle continued to be assembled worldwide, at plants in places as far away as Uruguay, Brazil, Mexico, Venezuela, Nigeria and, as shown here, Peru. The Peruvian plant had been established in 1966.

wheels. There was even a heated rear window fitted to the folding roof. Just two were offered to each dealer and many took this to mean that this was the Beetle's swan-song in the USA. It very nearly was.

In 1979 there would be no further changes made to the Beetle, although once again there would be a special edition cabriolet sold on the American market. This was the "Epilog" (sic) which was supplied in Henry Ford's favourite color scheme of any color you like as long as it's black. This time there was only one issued to each dealer and it really was the Beetle's swan-song in the US market, as the Mexican-built Beetles were never "Federalized" so as to be legal for sale in North America. They met neither the emission nor safety regulations current in the USA and

Below: The Epilog cabriolet was another special edition built for the US market. In stark contrast to the Triple White model, the Epilog was finished all in black. Note the fuel-injected engine's single exhaust tailpipe and the discreet badging on the deck lid. Widened wheel rims are a non-standard feature on this example.

THE THING

Above: Conceived as a military vehicle, the Type 181 was offered to the civilian market as the Thing in the USA, and the Trekker in most other countries. It was a simple, rugged vehicle aimed at the youth market.

Left: Although the Type 181 sold well in the USA, it always appeared to be a fish out of water in Europe, where the climate was somewhat against it.

Below: Despite stiff opposition from far more fuel-efficient cars, the Beetle entered the 1980s bloodied but unbeaten. Only rarely have photographs appeared showing the Beetle in a wind-tunnel, but it is interesting to note the excellent air-flow over this 1975 model. The Beetle had a Cd (coefficient of drag) of 0.44 which, while hardly placing it in the realms of Audi's highly-efficient 100 with its Cd of 0.34, was still better than the K70's 0.51!

remained a dream as far as American enthusiasts were concerned.

Finally, on January 10th, 1980, the very last Beetle cabriolet drove off the production line at Karmann and straight into the factory museum to take pride of place. There had been 331,850 cabriolets built since production began in 1949 with by far the greatest number finding their way to the USA. It was a black day indeed for Volkswagen fans the world over, for this meant that no longer was it possible to buy a Beetle that had been assembled anywhere in Europe.

Production still continued apace in many places throughout the world, however, Mexico remaining the source of all new Beetles as far as Germany was concerned. The model was still being assembled in Peru, Uruguay, Brazil, Venezuela, Nigeria, the Philippines and, until 1979, South Africa. It is ironic that, when the factory management made the decision to stop building the Beetle in Germany in 1978, domestic sales rose by some 55 percent as the Mexican version became available. Perhaps its was a sign that the customer really had not been impressed with all the MacPherson strut suspension, IRS rear ends, bulbous windshields, fancy ventilation systems and seemingly endless gimmicky special editions. Perhaps all he wanted was a basic, reliable, no fuss Beetle, just like the one he used to be able to buy. Or perhaps it was just a hint of nostalgia… After all, it always seems to be human nature to want something you can't have any more.

Although the last German sedan may have been built in 1978, the cabriolet continued to be produced at Osnabrück until January 10th, 1980 – almost two years to the day after the last sedan left Emden. It is a measure of the cabriolet's importance to Volkswagen that it remained in production for so long after the basic Beetle. The majority of these cars found their way to export markets, notably the USA where there was still a steady market. However, the writing was on the wall for the Beetle as far as Germany was concerned, for all thoughts had now turned towards production of the water-cooled cars: Golf, Scirocco and Polo.

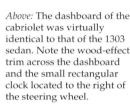

SPECIFICATIONS

Engine: Horizontally opposed, air-cooled four cylinder. **Construction:** Two-piece cast magnesium-alloy crankcase split vertically with separate cast-iron cylinders and cast aluminum alloy pistons. Four main bearings. Cast aluminum cylinder heads with separate inlet ports. **Bore and stroke:** 85.5mm x 69mm. **Capacity:** 1584cc (96.6ci). **Valves:** Pushrod operated overhead. **Compression ratio:** 7.5:1. **Fuel system:** Bosch AFC fuel-injection system. **Maximum power:** 50bhp (53 US hp) at 4,200rpm. **Maximum torque:** 72lb ft at 2,800rpm.

Transmission: Fully-synchromesh, four-speed manual transaxle with integral final drive unit. One-piece casing. **Gear ratios:** First – 3.78; second – 2.06; third – 1.32; fourth – 0.89; reverse – 3.79. **Final drive ratio:** 4.125 :1.

Brakes: Hydraulically-operated discs (front), drums (rear)

Steering: Rack and pinion.

Suspension: Front: Fully independent with MacPherson strut coil springs and dampers. Steering damper. **Rear:** Fully independent four-jointed with twin solid torsion bars, rear stabilizer bar and telescopic dampers.

Wheels and tires: 4.5J x 15in pressed steel wheels. 6.00 x 15 cross-ply tires.

Dimensions: Length: 4150mm (13ft 7.4in). **Width:** 1549mm (5ft 1in). **Height:** 1501mm (4ft 11in). **Wheelbase:** 2400mm (7ft 10.5in). **Dry weight:** 870kg (1918lb).

Peformance: Maximum speed: 135km/h (84mph). **Acceleration:** 0-96km/h (60mph): 18.4sec. **Fuel consumption:** 8.8lits/100km (32mpg).

Number built: (1979) 19,569 – Cabriolets

Owner: Edward Belcher

Below: In order to meet the stringent anti-emission regulations ("smog laws") in the USA, Volkswagen equipped the Beetle engine with a complex fuel-injection system. The system was not the success Volkswagen had hoped for, resulting in increased fuel consumption. Long-term reliability was also brought into question.

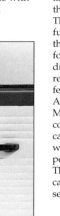

Above: The dashboard of the cabriolet was virtually identical to that of the 1303 sedan. Note the wood-effect trim across the dashboard and the small rectangular clock located to the right of the steering wheel.

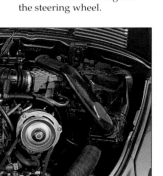

Below: The interior trim was little different to that of the last of the sedan models, with the exception of the color choice. Special versions of the cabriolet were available with all-white interiors and matching tops.

Below: In many ways, the last of the cabriolets were some of the most elegant of all Beetles. The curved windshield somehow seemed to suit the lines of the cabriolet better than it did those of the sedan. The top frame had been further redesigned to allow the top to sit lower when folded, thereby giving the driver a better view to the rear. Headrests were another feature dictated by the American safety lobby. Metallic paintwork and a pale colored top gave these late cabriolets a distinctive look which made them appeal to people from every walk of life. They were indeed a classless car and a classic in every sense.

Above: To meet American safety regulations, the Beetle was equipped with so-called "5mph impact" bumpers, designed to withstand a low-speed knock.

Above left & right: From the rear, the most obvious sign of change was the single exhaust tailpipe and the discreet "Fuel

Left: Late-model cabriolets were equipped with this combined mirror and interior courtesy light.

Injection" badging. At the front, note the air-intake grille under the front bumper – this was provided to allow air into

the optional air-conditioning system, which was mounted behind the valance at the rear of the car.

Right: Once again, the turn signals could be found located on the top of the front fenders on this 1979 model.

Above: Sports wheels were fitted to many of the last cabriolets to leave the production line. Note how the top could be raised but all the side glass lowered for a pillarless look.

With Beetle production halted in Europe, all eyes turned towards South America. Sales prospects here looked good – the poor road systems and lack of adequate public transport suggested that there was a large potential market for a ruggedly built, low-cost vehicle in South America. Government support was also available to help finance the enterprise. At Puebla, in Mexico, an assembly plant had been established in 1954, when just 500 Beetles were built from CKD kits (CKD = Completely Knocked Down – i.e., an entire car supplied in component form). The policy of supplying CKD Beetles was to prove popular for Volkswagen as it was a way in which its products could be imported into certain countries without flouting local trade restrictions. Several countries had, by now, imposed a limit on imports in an effort to encourage local industry and thereby bolster their flagging post-war economies.

Mexican-assembled Beetles proved popular on the home market, with sales growing steadily throughout the 1950s. Their success, however, attracted the attention of the Mexican government which, fearing

Above: The Volkswagen plant at Puebla, in Mexico, was opened in 1954 to cater for the potentially-large domestic market. While Wolfsburg would only build Beetles for a further 20 years, Puebla would continue to do so well into the 1990s.

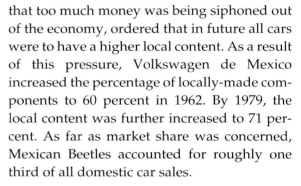

Left: This aerial view of the Puebla plant gives a clear impression of its sheer size. While lacking the character of Wolfsburg, with its famous chimneys, Puebla has all the hallmarks of a modern, efficient factory.

Below: A Mexican dealership in the 1980s, showing the variety of vehicles in use: Golfs and Beetles rub shoulders on the roof, while a pair of Brasilias can be seen at the far end of the forecourt. In the background, a VW Type 2 slowly climbs the hill past the dealership.

that too much money was being siphoned out of the economy, ordered that in future all cars were to have a higher local content. As a result of this pressure, Volkswagen de Mexico increased the percentage of locally-made components to 60 percent in 1962. By 1979, the local content was further increased to 71 percent. As far as market share was concerned, Mexican Beetles accounted for roughly one third of all domestic car sales.

Back To Germany

As we have seen, when Beetle production finally came to a halt in Germany, firstly at Wolfsburg and then Emden, Volkswagen made the slightly ironic decision to re-import the car from Mexico. Demand was high, despite the relatively low specification of the Mexican models, which came with the basic 1200cc 40hp engine, swing-axle rear and torsion bar front suspension and a flat windshield. However, the interior trim was slightly improved, with modern checkered upholstery and mildly revised instrumenta-

El Volkswagen. Reflejo de la perfección.

El Volkswagen.
Lo mejor compra.

Above: VW head Carl Hahn (right) meeting President Salinas of Mexico. For Mexico, the Beetle was a vital link in the country's economy, a point not lost on its political leaders. The car shown is the 20,000,000th Beetle – made in Mexico, naturally.

Left: This sales brochure for the Mexican-built Beetle looks remarkably like any produced in Germany during the 1970s. The imagery – a happy family group with their Volkswagen – was the same as that used in the original KdF-Wagen sales literature.

tion. The price was also attractive; it worked out at some 8 percent less than the last of the German-built Beetles.

Although the overall appearance of the Mexican Beetle was more impressive than the last of the German-assembled examples, with chromed hubcaps and bumpers and an attractive range of colors, the general feeling has always been that they never quite matched up to the quality of the Wolfsburg- or Emden-built cars. Maybe that's nostalgia coming to the fore, or maybe it really was the case. Whatever, for anyone who wished to buy a new Beetle in Europe, there was only one choice, take it or leave it.

20 Million Beetles!

The greatest landmark of all in Volkswagen's history occurred on May 15th, 1981, when the 20,000,000th Beetle rolled off the line at Puebla. To celebrate this occasion, a special range of Beetles was offered for sale, each finished in silver with a commemorative plaque proclaiming the new sales record. The following year, on November 11th, the 20,000,000th vehicle to be built at Wolfsburg was completed but, alas, this was a Golf Turbo Diesel.

The Mexican Beetle continued to be sold in Germany, with annual sales exceeding 17,500, until August 20th, 1985, when the last shipment arrived. The event was celebrated, for want of a better word, by a series of special "Jubilee" models which were built to mark the fiftieth anniversary of the Beetle, for it was back in 1935 that the Beetle project had first seen the light of day. Who could ever have expected the humble People's Car to have survived the war, become the number one best-selling car of all time and still be on sale half a century later? The Beetle was even

Above: The rugged nature of the Beetle makes it ideal for the rough terrain which can be found in South America. The photo shows a factory test car undergoing appraisal.

Left: Throughout Mexico the Beetle is regularly used as a taxi. Indeed, Beetle taxis far outnumber any other model, including Mercedes.

Right: "Volkswagen of Mexico continues with its program of exporting vehicles to Europe" reads the banner on the side of the ship. Long after the production lines in Germany had fallen silent, Mexican-built cars continued to be shipped to Europe aboard huge VW-owned merchant vessels, such as this.

The Beetle may have ground to a halt in Germany but in South America there was still a steadily increasing demand for this no-frills transportation. Production continued apace at the Puebla plant, soon to be followed, once again, by production in Brazil. These South American Beetles may not have quite the charm and simplicity – or, it can be argued, the build quality – of their German brethren, but they are Beetles through and through. Modern laws have forced such things as fuel-injection (Brazil) and safety steering-wheels on them but beneath the surface lie the traditional VW values of simplicity, ruggedness, reliability and economy.

Below: There is little to distinguish the South American Beetles from their European brethren for, at first sight, they appear to be identical to the average 1970s Beetle.

Above: The interior trim was somewhat more luxurious than the average European Beetle, with a brushed velour material being used on the seats. Note the plastic-covered dashboard and the unique steering wheel design.

SPECIFICATIONS

Engine: Horizontally opposed, air-cooled four cylinder. **Construction:** Two-piece cast magnesium-alloy crankcase split vertically with separate cast-iron cylinders and cast aluminum alloy pistons. Four main bearings. Cast aluminum cylinder heads with siamesed inlet ports. **Bore and stroke:** 77mm x 69mm. **Capacity:** 1584cc (96.6ci). **Valves:** Pushrod operated overhead. **Compression ratio:** 6.6:1. **Fuel system:** Mechanical fuel pump; single Brosol downdraft carburetor. **Maximum power:** 44bhp (53 US hp) at 4,000rpm. **Maximum torque:** 72lb ft at 2,000rpm.

Transmission: Fully-synchromesh, four-speed manual transaxle with integral final drive unit. One-piece casing. **Gear ratios:** First – 3.80; second – 2.06; third – 1.32; fourth – 0.89; reverse – 3.88. **Final drive ratio:** 4.375 :1.

Brakes: Hydraulically-operated drums on all four wheels

Steering: Worm and roller

Suspension: Front: Fully independent with transverse, multi-leaf torsion bars and telescopic dampers. Ball-joint design with hydraulic steering damper. **Rear:** Fully independent swing-axle with twin solid torsion bars and telescopic dampers.

Wheels and tires: 4J x 15in pressed steel wheels. 155 x 15 radial-ply tires.

Dimensions: Length: 4060mm (13ft 3.8in). **Width:** 1550mm (5ft 1in). **Height:** 1500mm (4ft 11in). **Wheelbase:** 2400mm (7ft 10.5in). **Dry weight:** 820kg (1808lb).

Peformance: Maximum speed: 127km/h (79mph). **Acceleration:** 0-96km/h (60mph): 22sec. **Fuel consumption:** 8.3lits/100km (34mpg).

Number built: Still in production

Owner: Volkswagen Mexico

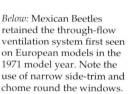

Below: Mexican Beetles retained the through-flow ventilation system first seen on European models in the 1971 model year. Note the use of narrow side-trim and chome round the windows.

Left: Sealed-beam headlamps and bumper-mounted turn signals gave the Mexican Beetle the appearance of a late-model European car. Bumpers are chrome-plated Europa-style.

Right: Rear light assemblies used on the Mexican Beetles are similar to those fitted to European-built models produced from 1973. The "elephants' feet" design is large enough to satisfy the most stringent regulations, even if the lights do little to enhance the vehicle's lines. Surrounds and housing are molded from plastic to reduce production costs.

Above left & right: From front or rear, there is little to distinguish this from any Beetle built in Germany.

Mexican Beetles were equipped with 1600cc engines which produced 53hp at 4,000rpm. The lowly 6.6:1 compression ratio allowed poor quality locally-refined fuel to be used without problem.

Right: Headrests were fitted as standard to comply with safety regulations worldwide. Note the door-mounted rear-view mirror and the rear-seat passenger grab strap.

Below: Until the reappearance of the Brazilian Beetle, this looked like it was to be the swan-song model. However, the Beetle refused to die and continued to be built into the late·1990s. Who knows, maybe it will outlast the rest of the Volkswagen range, including the Concept 1 New Beetle?

voted "Car Of The Century" by the world's motoring press in 1990, following a survey held by the French magazine *Auto Moto*. Mexican Beetles are still sold in Germany through specialist outlets, although they are no longer available through VW dealerships. They were even available at one point via a chain of supermarkets.

While Beetles continued to be produced in Mexico, another chapter in its remarkable history was about to open. The story really begins forty years earlier, in 1950, when José Thompson, head of Brasmotor, the Chrysler importer for Brazil, became intrigued by the Beetle and enquired whether he might be able to sell the car in South America. His initial approaches to Wolfsburg were unsuccessful, but his persistence paid off in 1949 when, through his friendship with C. T. Tomaz, head of Chrysler, Thompson was able to establish contact with Heinz Nordhoff. Nordhoff visited Brazil with his colleague, Friedrich Schultz-Wenk. Once there, Nordhoff could not fail to be impressed by Thompson's enthusiasm, or by the potential he recognized in the market, and he agreed to help set up an assembly plant in Brazil.

A New Factory

The first fruit of this liaison was a series of Beetles completed in 1953 at a rented industrial shed in Ipiranga, a suburb of São Paulo, the cars having again been supplied in CKD form from Germany. Between 1953 and 1957, a total of 2,268 Beetles and 552 Type 2s were assembled at São Paulo. However, in 1957, permission was granted to build a new factory which would allow full domestic manufacture of Volkswagens, thereby helping the Brazilian economy by reducing the number of imports. Indeed, until this plant was built, Brazil had to rely entirely on imported vehicles. In 1951, for example, the total expenditure on imported cars was some $276,500,000 and the average annual expenditure on vehicle imports during the 1950s was around $130,000,000. Such was the government's concern about the situation that a committee, GEIA (Automobile Industry's Export Group), headed by Lúcio Meira, was established in June 1956, with a brief to investigate ways round this imbalance between imports and exports.

That same year, Volkswagen do Brazil began work on building a new 10,000m² (107,600sq ft) assembly plant, located some 23km (14 miles) from São Paulo on the Via Anchieta, a road which linked the city with the port of Santos. However, it was not until September 2nd the following year that the first vehicle – a Type 2 – was completed, with the first Beetle not seeing the light of day until January 3rd, 1959. This car was purchased only four days later by Eduardo Matarazzo for

Above: The 20,000,000th Beetle rolled off the production line in Puebla on May 15th, 1981. A unique Silver Edition Beetle was launched to celebrate this latest milestone.

Left: The interior of the commemorative Jubilee Beetle was more modern than most, with striped fabric seating and a Golf steering wheel.

Below: The celebratory model came with discreet "20 Million" badging and a certificate to confirm its provenance. Original examples are much prized.

Left: Carl Hahn speaking at a special dinner held in honor of the Beetle's 50th birthday. Note the use of Beetle hoods as desks (lower left of the photo).

Right: Ivan Hirst signs the hood of the 50th anniversary Beetle which would then be put on display in the Wolfsburg Museum.

Above left & right: To celebrate the Beetle's half-centenary, Volkswagen launched the Jubilee model. This was finished in deep metallic silver with a small

"50 Jahre Käfer" badge on the deck lid. Only time will tell if there will ever be a "100 Jahre Käfer" to join it. If there is, it will probably be built in South America.

Below: In the 1980s, VW stopped exporting the Beetle to Europe – shown here is the last shipment to leave Mexico – but such was the demand that several dealers

imported them for customers. In the mid-1990s, it was possible to buy a new Beetle in Germany from a number of sources, including supermarkets.

the sum of Cr$471,200 from the Marcas Famosas dealership in São Paulo.

Despite having been in operation for almost two years, the plant was not officially opened until November 18th, 1959, by President Juscelino Kubitschek and São Paulo State Governor, Prof. Carvalho Pinto. Also in attendance were Wolfsburg chief, Heinz Nordhoff, and Friedrich Schultz-Wenk, who had been appointed head of Volkswagen do Brazil. Over the next twelve months, some 8,406 Beetles would be sold in Brazil and, by 1962, it had become the number one selling car, with a total of 31,014 units sold. On July 4th, 1967, the 500,000th Beetle – or Fusca, as it became officially known in Brazil – was built at the São Paulo plant. In line with Brazilian government policy, these domestically-built Beetles had a local content of 54 percent.

New Models

In June 1968, Rudolph Leiding took over the factory from Schultz-Wenk and was himself replaced by Werner P. Schmidt in 1971, when he returned to Wolfsburg to oversee the introduction of several new models. During Schmidt's reign, a number of new vehicles were added to the range, including the Brazilian equivalent of the Type 3 sedan, a Variant and in 1970 the so-called Fuscão, a Beetle with a larger 1500cc engine. Later, Schmidt would add the sporting Type 4-engined SP-2 and the highly-successful Brasilia hatchback before being replaced himself in July 1973 by Wolfgang Sauer. Sauer was credited with consolidating Volkswagen's domination of the domestic market at the same time as increasing the company's share of export sales.

In 1972, a total of 223,453 locally-manufactured Beetles were sold – that's an average of some 18,600 per month – which accounted for almost half of all vehicles sold on the Brazilian market. A further 6,000 Fuscas were also exported and, by March 1972, the total production of the model reached the 1,000,000 mark. Two years later, sales had climbed to 237,323, of which 24,474 were sent abroad, while June 1976 saw the 2,000,000th Brazilian Beetle leave the assembly line. There appeared to be no stopping the success of the Fusca, with exports reaching no fewer than 60 countries around the world.

Falling Demand

However, demand for the Beetle began to fall slowly as the nation became more affluent and Brazilians began to buy better-equipped cars. With sales dropping to just 34,000 units in 1984, the decision was made to halt production of the Beetle, although other models continued to be built. The last Beetle left São Paulo on December 7th, 1986, making a grand total of 3,300,000 built between 1959 and 1986. During this time, the Fusca had developed from a basic 1200cc model to a 1600cc, dual-carburetor, alcohol-fuelled sedan with disc brakes and rear stabilizer bar. This, perhaps, is the sort of model which Volkswagen in Germany should have built instead of the less-than-successful 1302 and 1303 models, but then hindsight is always perfect.

Ironically, one of the reasons behind the Beetle's demise in Brazil – the increasing affluence of the people – was partly responsible for its amazing reintroduction some eight years later. The government, led by President Itamar Franco, became acutely aware that

Right: The attractive SP-2 was a sports car built in Brazil, largely for the domestic market, although some examples did find their way abroad in the hands of private owners.

Below: The Brasilia was a vehicle unique to the Brazilian market and resembled a cross between the VW 412 and a Type 3 Variant (Squareback).

there was a large sector of the population which, although unable to afford an expensive car, was in a position to buy a basic vehicle, should one be available. With the loss of the Beetle from the Volkswagen range, there was no suitable low-cost model. Similarly, more affluent families, who wished to own a second or third car, were unable to buy the Beetles they wanted. There was also the small matter of inexpensive Japanese imported cars swamping the country, to the detriment of the economy. According to Rainer Wolf, executive manager in charge of Volkswagen's South American marketing division, market research showed that the new owner was most likely to be a male, 40+ years of age and married; he would be conservative in his tastes and have an eye for value for money.

Above: Brazilian Beetles produced in the 1970s were an odd amalgam of old and new styling. Note the small side windows but the upright headlamps and Europa bumpers.

Right: When the new Brazilian Beetle, or Fusca, was launched in 1993, an attractive sales brochure spoke eloquently of its modest virtues.

Below: "The Last of the First" could be the title of this 1986 photograph showing what was believed to be the last Beetle to leave Brazil. Who would have expected production to recommence seven years later?

Fusca.
As boas idéias são simples.

A New Beginning

On February 4th, 1993, following pressure from President Franco, the Brazilian government signed a document, called a Protocol Of Intent, allowing the state-funded car industry, Autolatina, to back the reintroduction of the Fusca to the tune of some $30,000,000. This lead to the creation of 800 new jobs at São Paulo, in addition to a further 24,000 as part of the massive infrastructure necessary to market and service the new cars. It was estimated that a total of 100,000 people would directly benefit from this program. A production target of 24,000 cars per year was set, with the reborn Beetle selling at the equivalent of $11,000; this figure included 0.1 percent Industrial Products Tax, 2 percent manufacturer's social security contribution and a corresponding 2 percent dealer contribution.

There was good reasoning behind the decision to reintroduce the Beetle, as opposed to designing an entirely new model, aside from the most obvious advantage of not having to manufacture new press tooling. For, despite Brazil's increasing affluence, the road system was still in a poor state and, of the estimated 1,500,000km (93,200 miles) of highways, only 9 percent were paved. This meant that for those people living outside the major conurbations, any car had to be capable of standing up to use in rugged conditions. With the exception of four-wheel-drive vehicles, the Beetle was the only car suited to the terrain.

The Final Chapter?

The new Beetle was assembled in an 8,000m² (86,000sq ft) wing of the Anchieta Industrial Unit at São Bernardo do Campo in São Paulo. The building housed a new, fully-automated production line which was a far cry from the original rented shed, where the CKD models were assembled at the very beginning of Beetle assembly in Brazil some 40 years earlier. The first completed car rolled off the line on August 23rd, 1993.

The Brazilian Beetle almost certainly represents the final chapter in the development of the People's Car as we know it and, as such, it is worth taking a detailed look at its specification. Based very much on the European models of the early 1970s, the Fusca was a flat-screen Beetle equipped with torsion bar front suspension and swing-axle rear. It was powered by a 1584cc engine, with dual Solex H32PDSIT carburetors and had a compression ratio of 10.0:1 to allow it to burn domestically-produced, wood-based, alcohol fuel. The result was a power output of 58.7hp (SAE) produced at 4,300rpm, with maximum torque

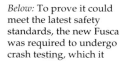

Below: To prove it could meet the latest safety standards, the new Fusca was required to undergo crash testing, which it passed with flying colors. Although a design which was now almost 60 years old, the Beetle proved to be as strong as any modern car.

Above left & right: The new Fusca still retains the smaller side windows last seen on European Beetles built prior to 1965. However, the remainder of the styling was brought up to date. At the rear, a VW badge appeared on the deck lid for the first time in the Beetle's history.

of 11.9kgfm (86lb/ft) at just 2,800rpm. In line with the then current emission laws, the exhaust system was fitted with a catalytic convertor located under the rear valance, with the main muffler being tucked up under the driver's-side rear fender. A single tailpipe exited under the wheel arch. The transmission was a special "sealed for life" version of the traditional four-speed manual transaxle fitted to the majority of Beetles since 1962. The dual-circuit braking system consisted of disc brakes on the front, with drums at the rear.

As far as interior trim was concerned, the Fusca came with a plastic padded dashboard (simply a cover fitted over the old pressed steel panel) into which was set a square speedometer, calibrated to 160km/h (100mph), the design of which seemed at odds with the car's rather old-fashioned styling. To the right of this was a fuel gauge, while to the left was space for an optional clock. The steering wheel was moulded from deformable black plastic, and looked similar to those fitted

Above: The Brazilian Gol was powered by a modified version of the Beetle engine, driving the front wheels.

Right: The Fusca features a dual-carburetor engine with a catalytic convertor to meet new anti-emission laws.

Left: The Gol was something of a strange hybrid, being a cross between a Beetle (engine) and the European VW Polo (styling).

Below right: As it approaches the millennium, the Beetle steadfastly refuses to lie down and die. Long live the Volkswagen Beetle!

to most Volkswagens in the 1970s. In the center of the horn push was a Volkswagen roundel logo. The seats were far better than anything previously offered in a basic Beetle, being trimmed in velour material with separate head restraints, reinforced frames and mountings and a reclining mechanism. Redesigned seat-belt anchorage points, front and back, further helped to improve passenger safety.

The factory claimed a 0-100km/h (0-62mph) time of just 14.5 seconds, with a maximum speed of 140km/h (87mph). The fuel economy was not ground-breaking by any means, with an average consumption of just 9km/l (approximately 25mpg), although it has to be remembered that this figure was achieved using extremely cheap alcohol-based fuel. It is interesting to note that the coefficient of drag (Cd) was stated as being 0.48, somewhat worse than the 0.44 figure claimed by Wolfsburg for its Beetle in the 1970s.

The Fusca was launched in a range of three standard colors – Star White, Arena Beige and Saturn Blue – along with five optional colors: Universal Black, Sports Red, Lunar Silver, Athenas Beige Metallic and Pine Green Metallic. In addition, two option packages were offered from the very beginning. Package 1 consisted of a clock, foam-covered sports steering wheel, dual horns, door pockets, a carpeted strip on the bottom of the door panels, protective rubber strips on the bumpers and a passenger-side door mirror. Package 2 added a heated rear window, green-tinted windows, opening rear-side windows, tinted rear light lenses and a digital stereo system.

This, then, was how the Beetle would see

out the 1990s – in many ways a far cry from the original, no-nonsense People's Car of the late 1930s, and yet, in other ways, so similar. After all, was it not the word of Germany's leader that led to the introduction of a cheap car for the masses, in the same way that, in 1993, the Brazilian President pushed for Volkswagen to reintroduce the Beetle to provide that same inexpensive transport for his people?

Full Circle

So, the Beetle lives on. The words of a somewhat confused official press release, issued on the reintroduction of the Fusca, could almost be those of a political speech made 60 years earlier in a restless Germany: "*As a popular car, it fits into the brand's renewal program, which heads an industrial policy that aims at the production of cars for all the social segments. In terms of its characteristics and cost-benefit advantages already experienced by the consumers, the Fusca will conquer its rightful niche within the market, a niche in which rationality and attributes that are considerably differentiated in relation to other models in the same line, predominate. Volkswagen's Marketing Planning Division envisages that the Fusca will win a 10 percent market share to begin with in the popular car segment, the average demand of which is estimated at between 20,000 and 25,000 units per year.*"

While the old Beetle may appear to have earned itself an honorable retirement, seeing out its twilight years in Mexico and Brazil, all thoughts regarding a modern replacement were firmly centered on the 1994 Detroit Motor Show. Here, much to everyone's amazement, Volkswagen chose to launch an eye-catching, cheeky little runabout with distinctly Beetle-like retro styling.

Instantly hailed by the world's press as the new Beetle, the prototype sedan was officially known as Concept 1. Its roots, however, are not to be found in Wolfsburg, nor even South America, but in California's Simi Valley. The project began life as an expression of the enthusiasm that two talented designers had for the original Beetle, in an age when all cars seem to look the same. The designers, Freeman Thomas and J. Carrol Mays, both trained at the American Art Center College of Design, after which they each moved to Europe. Mays joined Audi as a designer while Thomas found a position at Porsche. In 1991, they returned to California to open a design center, called the American Design Center, for Volkswagen and Audi.

Above: The Chico was just one of Volkswagen's many prototypes built over the years which addressed the matter of a small car for the future. A change of heart among the Volkswagen management stopped the project at the last moment.

The Concept 1 is, without doubt, the project which put them on the map, although soon after its announcement, Mays returned to Audi to head its design department.

Concept 1 was not the result of a commission from Volkswagen to design a new car for

Mays and Thomas were aware of the problems which faced Volkswagen and also of the fact that so many modern cars are characterless. They are designed by computer, tested in wind tunnels and roll off the production line in their millions every year. What Volkswagen needed, according to the two California-based stylists, was a car that would stand out from that crowd, which would have the timeless charm of the original Beetle and which would thrust the company back into the limelight. Although Concept 1 certainly did that when it was launched at the Detroit Motor Show in January 1994, few people honestly expected the design to see production. Even Volkswagen representatives on the stand suggested that it was little more than a whimsical styling exercise: a "what if…?" concept vehicle which was intended to prove that Volkswagen was still capable of keeping one step ahead of the pack.

Enthusiastic Response

What no-one expected, though, was the amazingly enthusiastic reaction to the car. The motoring press, usually so skeptical and cynical about such exercises, was universal in its praise for the design, although many journalists felt that such a car would not be the answer to Volkswagen's long-term problems. It would, at best, be an interesting diversion. Shortly after, Volkswagen itself began speaking of the possibility of building a limited number of such cars, but remained somewhat non-committal about the subject.

Public reaction, however, was overwhelming – the VW stand was mobbed throughout the show by people wanting to know when Concept 1 was going into production. Volkswagen dealers in the USA reported a steady increase in "traffic" through their showrooms as people came to enquire when the new model was going to be available. The public was demanding a car that allowed its owner to make a personal statement and through which he or she could express his or her individuality, citing the Beetle as the perfect example of this. It is rather ironic that the old Beetle should have been viewed this way. After all, it could be argued that how can a car, of which over 20,000,000 examples have been built, allow its owner to stand out from a crowd? Mays and Thomas had always spoken of four words which they felt summed up the project: simple, reliable, honest and original. Perhaps those were four virtues which the public found lacking in other cars currently on the market. Indeed, these were the four words around which the color brochure – now a much sought-after collector's item – centered when VWoA issued it at Detroit.

This brochure makes interesting reading, for it includes several references to the origi-

Above: When first exhibited at the 1994 Detroit Motor Show, Concept 1 stopped people in their tracks.

Right: Volkswagen adopted this simple logo to identify the Concept 1 project. Even from this it is easy to see the relationship with the Beetle.

Below: The Detroit show brochure was a work of art in itself. Exquisitely photographed, many references to the original Beetle appeared in its text. There was much talk of friendships rekindled and plenty of "remember when…?" phraseology.

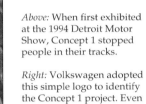

Left: Concept 1 was the brainchild of two men: Freeman Thomas and J. Carrol Mays. Thomas and Mays worked at the Volkswagen of America Design Center at Simi Valley, California, where they drew up plans for a small car which would capture the spirit of the original Beetle. With several design references to the old car, such as the vestigial horn grilles on the front fenders, the car soon won the hearts of all that saw it.

the millennium. Engineers at Wolfsburg had already progressed a long way down that road with a vehicle of their own by the time Concept 1 appeared. In fact, theirs would be the second small car project with which Volkswagen hoped to halt its flagging sales world-wide. The first was known by its working title of Chico, a compact town car which fitted into the current range under the Polo. The Chico was almost at the point of going into production when the plug was pulled on the project after senior management began to have severe reservations about its viability. Aside from being an expensive mistake, the Chico was also an acute embarrassment for Volkswagen. Concept 1 offered the company an opportunity to divert attention away from the errors of the past.

Following the display of the original sedan Concept 1 in 1994, Volkswagen exhibited an attractive cabriolet prototype at the Geneva Motor Show in March 1995. The response from the public was overwhelming, convincing VW that the project was worth pursuing. Although the new car was not destined to go into production until the end of 1997, it was officially given a name in 1996: The New Beetle. It will be assembled in the VW plant at Puebla in Mexico, with the majority of production finding its way into the United States and Japan. There is no denying there is still a hint of the old Karmann-built Beetle cabriolets about this exciting vehicle.

Above: In profile, references to the Beetle were obvious: the running boards, separate fenders, large wheels and the flowing lines. Classic Beetle.

Left: Huge 17 inch aluminium wheels featured the traditional VW logo in the center, just like the original Beetle hubcap of the 1950s and '60s.

Left: The dashboard was a masterpiece of retro styling. The speedometer was an obvious reference to that of the Beetle, while the design of the steering wheel had hints of the 1960s about it, with a vestigial horn ring concealing the air-bag.

Right: The Concept 1 cabriolet is, perhaps, the more attractive of the two design exercises. Its retains the flowing lines of the sedan yet captures the chic good looks of the original Beetle cabriolet. Large diameter wheels with low-profile tires bring the design right up to date.

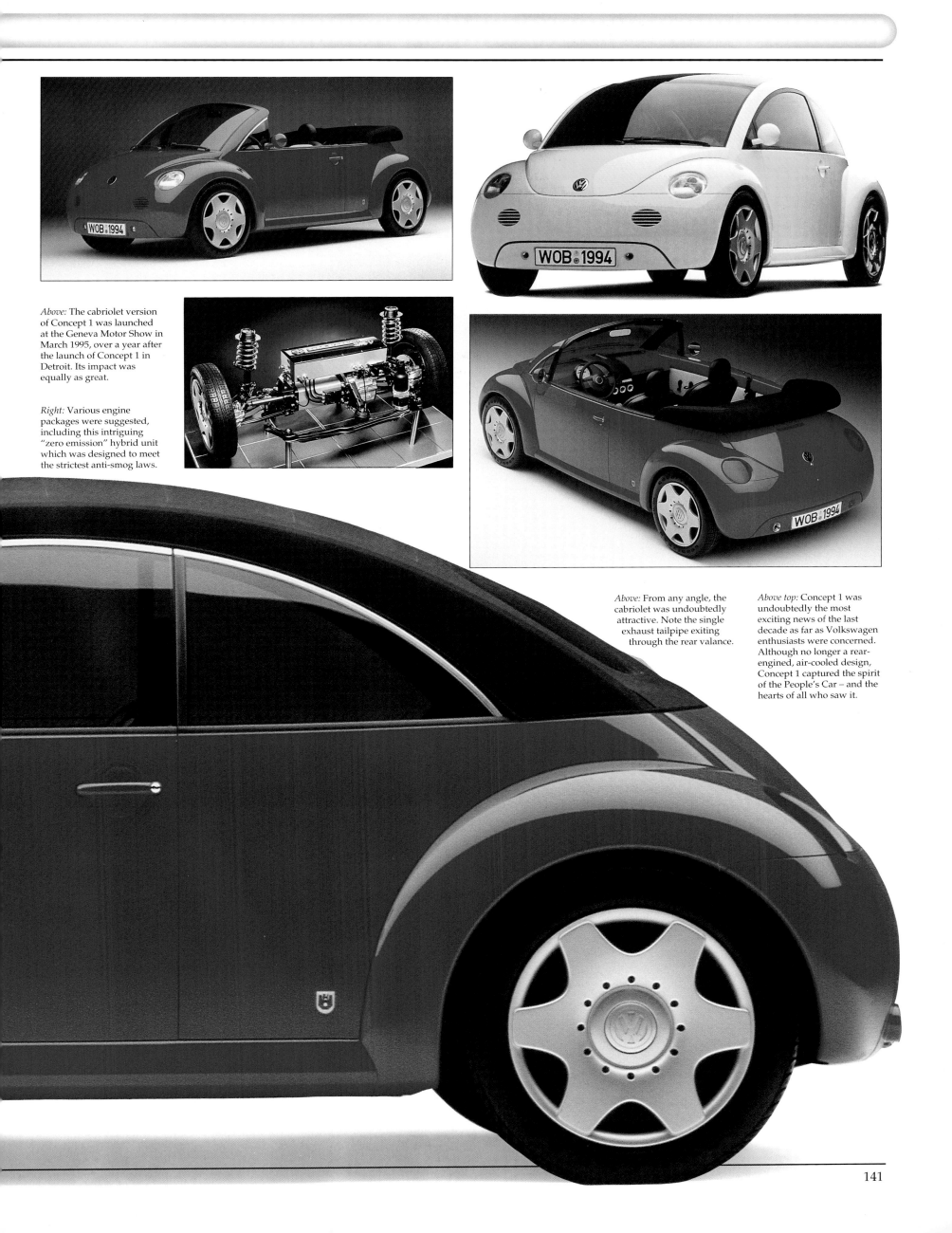

Above: The cabriolet version of Concept 1 was launched at the Geneva Motor Show in March 1995, over a year after the launch of Concept 1 in Detroit. Its impact was equally as great.

Right: Various engine packages were suggested, including this intriguing "zero emission" hybrid unit which was designed to meet the strictest anti-smog laws.

Above: From any angle, the cabriolet was undoubtedly attractive. Note the single exhaust tailpipe exiting through the rear valance.

Above top: Concept 1 was undoubtedly the most exciting news of the last decade as far as Volkswagen enthusiasts were concerned. Although no longer a rear-engined, air-cooled design, Concept 1 captured the spirit of the People's Car – and the hearts of all who saw it.

nal Beetle, something which no VW marketing material had done for many years. Indeed, Volkswagen had succeeded in alienating Beetle fans with a television advert which showed, in the background, a Beetle being dropped onto the ground from a great height as if in a gesture to say "what's past is past."

"Simply Unforgettable"

The wording of the brochure neatly summarizes the whole philosophy behind Concept 1: *"Simple: It's funny the things we remember. The things we hang on to. The first day of school. A first dance, a first kiss. Our first car. Some things are simply unforgettable. Reliable: One little thing can bring it all rushing back. A song on the radio. The smell of suntan lotion. Seeing an old friend at the beach. The friend you could always depend on. Honest: Everything was a little less complicated then. Tennis shoes didn't cost $200. A jukebox played your favorite song. And a car was part of the family. Right from the start. Original: What if quality never went out of style? What if originality still meant something original? What if simplicity, honesty and reliability came back again? Imagine. Imagine a new Volkswagen. A concept that redefines the automotive icon. Imagine a vision of high technology and advanced engineering. An expression of innovation, safety and performance. Imagine the descendant of an enduring original. Different, unmistakable, yet true to its heritage in style and in spirit. Every line, every curve, every memory. Not just the evolution of a cherished classic, but the continuation of a world-wide love affair that began 21 million cars ago. Innovation embodied in tradition. A new Volkswagen concept. One look and it all comes back. But then, it never really left. The legend reborn. A friendship rekindled."*

At the same time as the publication of this brochure, Volkswagen of America released a promotional video of Concept 1 to its dealers, which repeated this text while showing a metamorphosing image of a Beetle becoming a Concept 1. The video is without doubt one of the best promotional films of all time. However, with its dramatic visual impact and, above all, its stirring music, it is not difficult to be reminded of early propaganda films made over fifty years ago which extolled the virtues of the People's Car.

Soon after the Detroit show, Volkswagen rocked the automobile world a second time by displaying a bright red Concept 1 cabriolet alongside the yellow sedan at Geneva in March 1995. By now, the public was delirious and crying for more of the same. Still Volkswagen kept tight-lipped about the whole project. It would be another year before the official word was out that, yes, a new car based on the Concept 1 project would be put into series production, and that it would be on sale before the end of the century. It seemed

Above: Late in 1995 Volkswagen released photographs of the second generation Concept 1 – a pre-production model which pointed the way to what the eventual production version would look like. The car looked stunning in black.

Right: From the front, some minor changes can be seen, compared with the original Concept 1 show car. Note the large air intake for the front-mounted radiator.

Below: The interior retained much of its predecessor's charm, although the instrumentation and controls had been made more suitable for everyday use.

careful consideration of several key factors. One was that Concept 1 should definitely appeal to all age groups and classes. The original Beetle is truly a classless car which is driven by people from all walks of life. A Beetle looks equally at home outside the Milan Opera House as it does in the back streets of São Paulo. There is no stigma or snobbery attached to ownership of a Beetle. This was something which Mays and Thomas were keen to capture with their new design. It had to have a certain simple, chic elegance which would appeal to everyone.

There is a long-held belief that everyone at sometime in their life has been in a Beetle – that experience more often than not leaving an indelible, but pleasant, mark on the memory. Again the two designers were anxious to capture this warm feeling that Beetles tend to engender in people who come into contact with them. People remember little things about the Beetle: the way it sounds, the look of the dashboard with its simple, single-dial styling, the cocoon-like atmosphere in the back seat, the grab handles for the passengers and, naturally, the unique, almost organic, styling. With Concept 1, from the word go, there was a conscious effort to recreate this friendly image. The dashboard is a simple design with a large single speedometer, a passenger grab handle and even a place to mount a small flower vase, just like the 1950s' accessory bud vases that were so popular.

Retro Styling

Externally, there are several design references to the original Beetle, such as the four separate fenders, the stylized "running boards" (in reality, they have more in common with modern ground-effects styling), the steeply sloping nose and the door handles, for instance. The headlamps are also reminiscent of the Beetle's, with sloping lenses which follow the angle of the front fenders. However, on Concept 1 they are canted slightly to the side so that they offer greater safety at night. On the design exercise, they also incorporated the turn signals and just below, and inset from, the headlamps could be seen a pair of vents which strongly resembled the horn grilles of the Beetle.

The roof line of Concept 1 is pure Beetle from whichever angle it is viewed – even the windshield has an air of the original about it, despite being deep and curved. In many ways, it is far less obtrusive to the design than that used on the 1303 range back in the early 1970s. The prototype used a glass roof insert, but this was painted in such a way that the sharply defined edges of this extravagant sun roof echoed the swage lines stamped into the Beetle's roof a few inches inboard of the rain channels. On production versions, the roof is,

Above: The rear three-quarter view remained the most attractive of all. The highly-polished aluminium wheels looked especially good.

Right: The rear lid may not have concealed an air-cooled engine, but the overall design was clearly reminiscent of Beetles built in the late 1970s.

Below: The headlamps could have been those of a Porsche but there was no mistaking the identity of the car when you saw the badge. Attention to design detail was extremely high.

that at least one major automobile manufacturer had a soul and was prepared to listen to what the public was saying. Indeed, in the USA, Volkswagen of America opened a toll-free telephone line – the number of which was 1-800-444-VWUS – on which the public could leave a message to express their feelings about Concept 1. Presumably, VWoA had set itself a target number of calls which, once exceeded, would mean giving the green light to Germany to go ahead with the project! For May and Thomas, this was vindication of all the effort they had put into the exercise.

Concept 1 is, in reality, far more than a 1990's reincarnation of the Beetle: it is a thoroughly modern car whose appearance has arisen, not only as the result of a desire to build a vehicle which echoed the lines of the world's most famous car, but also as a result of in fact, solid as the cost of incorporating a full glass panel proved prohibitive. As far as the cabriolet version was concerned, with the hood folded down, there was that familiar bustle at the back which was such a distinctive trademark of all Beetle cabrios from 1949 right up until the last model rolled off the line in January 1980. It was almost possible to imagine workers at the Karmann factory nodding their heads in approval.

At the rear, the exhaust tailpipe, exiting through the rear valance, suggested a hint of the Beetle's exhaust system, while the rear lights had a distinct touch of the later "elephant's feet" units seen on mid-seventies models. On each quarter panel, ahead of the rear wheel arches, Concept 1 proudly displayed a stylized version of the traditional Wolfsburg crest, recessed into the body. On the nose and tail, the universally-recognized circular VW logo was similarly sunk into the bodywork.

However, what will not be seen on Concept 1 are the separate bumpers that were so much part of the original Beetle's styling. These made way for deformable units that would withstand parking knocks without damage. With regard to the matter of how such a car could be designed to meet the stringent safety regulations in operation round the world, Mays and Thomas incorporated a safety cell into the curvaceous body, with strengthening beams in the doors, roll-over protection in the roof and crumple zones at the front and rear.

Above: As the "New Beetle," as it had been dubbed by Volkswagen, neared production, there was still talk of several possible drivetrains, including this 1.9-liter turbo-diesel. As the new car was to be based on the floorpan of the latest model] Golf, there was even talk of a sporting version, powered by the legendary 2.8-liter VR6 engine. That would, indeed, be guaranteed to raise a smile!

Below: The production version of the New Beetle was very similar to the black prototype seen a year or so earlier. Sadly, some of the more stylish elements had disappeared, such as the round door mirrors and tube-like door handles, but the overall image was much the same. It was hard for Beetle enthusiasts to believe that the car was about to go into production, five years after Concept 1 first appeared.

The most significant area in which Concept 1 differs from the Type 1 is in the choice of drivetrain. At the time of its "launch" at Detroit and subsequently in Geneva, by which time the company was making veiled references to a production version, the plan was to make use of the floorpan and front-wheel-drive driveline from the next generation Volkswagen Polo. There was even talk of three environmentally-friendly power trains: a 1.9-

liter turbo diesel as introduced in the Mk3 Golf; a hybrid 1.4-liter, three-cylinder turbo diesel combined with an 18kW electric motor for town use; and an all-electric version using a 50bhp induction motor developed by the Siemens electrical company. Clearly Concept 1 was to be a ground-breaking exercise.

Above left & right: From 1948 to 1998. These two cars may be half a century apart, but there are undeniable links. Hints of Hermann Walter's Type 1 – separate wings, headlights, shape of the bonnet – can still be seen in the New Beetle.

Right: Sadly, a little of the original Concept 1's style had been lost as the car approached production. However, the interior still retained most of design elements which made the prototype so special.

Into Production

However, by the time the second revised prototype was shown in Japan during 1995, there was definite confirmation that the model was to go into production towards the end of the century. By now, there had been a shift in thinking, with the new car due to be based on the next generation Golf floorpan. This resulted in a slightly longer wheelbase and an increased range of drivetrain options, up to and including the superb narrow-angle VR6 engine package which drew much acclaim on its introduction in the Mk3 Golf, Vento (Jetta in the USA) and Passat vehicles. As far as suspension is concerned, Concept 1 is equipped with MacPherson struts at the front and a compound beam axle at the rear. While the strut front suspension is reminiscent of that fitted to the 1302 and 1303 Super Beetles of the seventies, the rear suspension is a major departure from the old swing-axles and torsion bars of thirty years earlier.

One area in which there is a similarity with the Beetle is the decision is to use large diameter wheels and tires – although the huge 18-inch diameter aluminium wheels of the original design exercise were clearly unlikely ever to see production. In fact, that first prototype paid little heed to many practicalities, such as suspension movement. There was simply insufficient clearance between the tires

and the wheel arches. However, by the time the second incarnation arrived, the wheel diameter had been reduced by 5cm (2in) and the tires down-sized accordingly. Large diameter wheels not only help to give better ride quality but also, according to Mays and Thomas, the original designers, give a vehicle an air of quality. After all, they maintain, if you see an entry-level car driving on 13-inch wheels, it looks like what it really is: a cheap car. Just because Concept 1 was not intended to be an expensive vehicle, that did not mean that it had to look cheap or lacking in style.

Although it would have been pleasingly romantic to imagine this new car being built at Wolfsburg, home all those years ago of the People's Car, the cold reality is that South America is the chosen "home" of Concept 1. The Volkswagen plant at Puebla in Mexico, itself long associated with the Beetle, is geared up to produce some 100,000 cars a year. The majority of these are destined for sale in the USA, where the traditional Beetle has not been

available for almost twenty years, thanks to stringent anti-emission and safety legislation. A considerable number will also find their way to Japan, another country which has a long-standing love affair with the Beetle. The remainder will be offered for sale in Europe, its spiritual home. The majority of these will be sold in Germany, leaving precious few available for other traditional European Beetle markets, such as Britain and France.

In 1996, the decision was taken to give the new car a name, "The New Beetle." This caused something of a stir amongst the traditional-thinking Beetle enthusiasts but, as far as Volkswagen was concerned, it appeared to be a case of "the King is dead, long live the King!" However, as any Beetle enthusiast will tell you, the difference is that the Beetle is not dead, at least not so long as it remains in production in South America. Perhaps Volkswagen should have kept the "Concept 1" title. After all, there will truthfully only ever be one Beetle…

Throughout the life of the Beetle, there have been many thousands of changes made in an effort to improve the product. Some have been significant, such as introducing a one-piece rear window in 1953, or a curved windshield late in 1972, while others have been relatively minor, such as fitting new dashboard knobs for 1967. In this appendix, we show several of the more important modifications made to the Volkswagen, including a look at the many engines which have been fitted over the years. Please note, however, that the year headings below the photographs refer to the particular vehicle shown, not necessarily the year any change was first made.

1956

1962

Locking mechanism was improved for this year. Cabriolet models featured a lock on the cable-release.

1960 had seen introduction of a new Wolfsburg badge, although design of hood handle was unchanged.

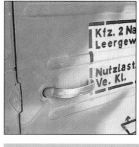

1944

1948

Design of the Kübelwagen was kept deliberately simple, with details like the door handles reflecting this.

The first post-war Beetles were little different from the original prototypes. Note recess in door for fingers.

1967

1968

The 1966/67 handles could still only be locked from the driver's side. These handles are now hard to locate.

To prevent the door opening in a roll-over accident, a trigger-operated lock was introduced this year.

HOOD HANDLES

The handle securing the front hood lid underwent two basic design changes throughout the fifty-year life of the Beetle. To begin with, the hood was secured with a handle which had to be turned to release the lock. Then, in 1949, the design was changed on export models to incorporate a more secure internal cable-release mechanism. This remained in use, basically unchanged, until 1968 when a push-button-operated safety catch was introduced.

1938

The pre-war VW38 came with this simple handle which needed to be turned counter-clockwise to release.

1943

The design remained unchanged by the time wartime production had started. Note the lock.

1948

This was the last year that the export models featured the old-style turn handle. Black was the regular finish.

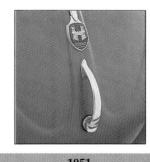

1951

In 1949, a cable-release mechanism offered security against theft. New handle is cast aluminum. Note badge.

1953

New chromium-plated handle was a consequence of an improvement in the supply of raw materials.

1966

The hood badge was deleted in October 1962, much to enthusiasts' sorrow. Handle and lock remained the same.

1968

Due to stricter safety laws, a new hood handle incorporated a secondary push-button safety catch.

1974

The design was little changed until 1970's when the push-button changed from chrome to black finish.

DOOR HANDLES

The design of the Beetle door handle underwent several changes throughout the car's life, many of them due to pressure from increasingly stringent safety laws introduced in the US. While it is true to say that some of the modifications were relatively minor and little more than cosmetic, others helped to prevent the door bursting open in a roll-over accident. For the restorer of an early Beetle, sourcing the correct door handles can be a difficult task.

1938

The black-finished, pull-handle design was first seen on the VW38 prototypes. Note the key-operated lock.

1943

In wartime, the Beetle featured handles which were painted body-color, in this instance, sand beige.

1951

July 1949 had seen the introduction of the export model with chromium-plated trim, including door handles.

1953

Driver's side was equipped with a key-operated lock. Passenger door was locked from inside the vehicle.

1956

The design of the handle, while superficially the same, changed in August 1955. Note subtle raised ridge.

1959

This was the last year of the old-style pull-handle, the design of which could be traced back over 20 years.

1962

In August 1959, an all-new push-button door lock was introduced, offering greater safety in an accident.

1966

In May 1966, a new door handle was fitted to all models, a design which was used for less than two years.

HEADLIGHTS

At first glance, there only appears to have been one redesign of the Beetle headlight assembly, this taking place in the mid-1960's when the old-style sloping headlamp was superseded by the new "upright" design. However, there have been many detail modifications over the years which can cause confusion among those wishing to restore a Beetle to its original specification. Different markets also often required different light assemblies.

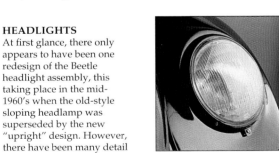

1938

Headlamps used on the VW38 were equipped with symmetrically-fluted lenses. Units used separate bulbs.

1943

The design remained unchanged for the first few years of production. Note body-colored rims.

1944

A headlamp of the Type 166 Schwimmwagen is shown here equipped with a black-out cover.

1944

The headlamps of the Type 82 Kübelwagen were similar. They were mounted atop each front fender.

1948

Hella headlamp units had adjusting screws located at the 8 o'clock and 4 o'clock positions on the rim.

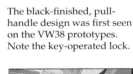

1951 | **1953** | **1957** | **1959** | **1966** | **1968**

Headlamp eyebrows were popular accessories which were designed to focus the light beam more efficiently.

Bosch headlamp units had the adjusting screws located at 12 o'clock and 9 o'clock. Lenses bore Bosch logos.

From April 1955, all US-spec Beetles were fitted with new headlamps which had clear lenses and a parking light.

On the European market, Beetles still came with symmetrical lenses to dip the lights straight down.

From August 1960, all Beetles, other than US-spec models, came with new asymmetrical lenses.

First seen on US Beetles in 1967, the upright headlamp was not universally adopted until 1968.

1943 | **1944** | **1948** | **1951** | **1953** | **1956**

The principal difference between this and the previous design was the use of a chrome lens surround.

Military vehicles were fitted with "convoy lights" which enabled following drivers to judge distance at night.

The design of the rear light remained essentially unchanged when civilian production first started.

In 1949 the chrome bezel was replaced by a smaller aluminum one, this itself being deleted in 1950.

In October 1952 the rear lights were redesigned to incorporate a brake light lens in the top of the housing.

In May 1955 a new rear light was introduced on the US market, which incorporated a turn signal.

WHEELS

One of the most recognizable features of the Beetle has always been the hubcap. The simple, chrome-plated, domed hubcap, which was used throughout the 1950s and for much of the 1960s, became almost as well-known as the profile of the Beetle itself. The wheels, too, have always been very distinctive in design, if rather plain by comparison with those of other makes of car, the large diameter being something of a Beetle trademark.

1968 | **1974** | **1938** | **1943** | **1944**

To meet stricter safety regulations, a larger rear light assembly was introduced in 1968.

The so-called "elephant's foot" or "football" rear light was first seen on the 1303 model in late 1972.

The VW38 models were fitted with plain black hubcaps which bore no logo of any description.

Military models rarely carried any form of embellishment. The 16-inch wheel is seen in all its glory.

The Type 166 Schwimmwagen was equipped with plain 16in wheels and off-road tyres.

1948 | **1951** | **1953** | **1956** | **1957** | **1962**

The first post-war Beetles came with domed hubcaps which featured a large VW logo stamped in the center.

With the introduction of the export models in 1949, a chromed hubcap with a small logo became available.

In October 1952 the wheel size was reduced to 15in. The design of the hubcap remained unchanged.

Cabriolets came from the factory with chrome trim rings fitted. Shown here is an accessory item.

Whitewall tires were never offered by the factory as a standard fitment. However, they were popular in the USA.

This was the last year that VWs came with a painted hubcap logo. From now on the hubcaps would be plain.

1974

Sealed-beam headlamp units were introduced across the range in September 1973. Note bulbous 1303 fender.

1975

Although the design remained unchanged, some late cars did feature plastic headlamp rims.

1957

The new unit was fitted to all models in August 1955, but semaphore turn signals remained on European cars.

1962

The first light unit to include a separate turn-signal lens was first seen in May 1961. US models had all-red lens.

1944

The Type 82 Kübelwagen could often be seen wearing these "nipple" hubcaps bearing the KdF logo.

REAR LIGHTS

Until the introduction of the much larger light clusters in 1962, the Beetle was constantly at risk from being rear-ended by vehicles following close behind at night. The small, rather dim, rear lights were never very efficient at the best of times, a short-coming made worse by an inadequate six-volt electrical system. In 1968, the light units were considerably increased in size, helping to make the Beetle a far safer car. Reversing lights also became available.

1938

Early rear lights consisted of small glass lenses set in a plain black bezel. The brake light was a separate unit.

1966

The flat hubcap used on the Type 3 models was fitted to the Beetle in 1966. Note correct cabriolet trim ring.

1967

With the availability of disc brakes from August 1966, a new, flatter hubcap was fitted. Note slotted wheels.

1968

The Beetle now came with four-bolt wheels, which required the use of the new flat hubcap.

1974

Sports wheels were fitted to several Beetles in the 1970s, varying in width from 4.5J to 5.5J, according to model.

1953

A new, smooth semaphore was featured on all oval-window models. The covers were painted body color.

1956

As there were no true door pillars, cabriolet models had the semaphores located in the rear quarter panels.

1957

For the US market, all 1956-1958 models featured small bullet-shaped turn signals located on front fender.

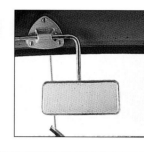

1943

The "football" mirror continued in use throughout the wartime period in the Type 82E and related models.

1948

The mirror was painted black up until 1949 and was secured to the bodywork with three small screws.

1951

In June 1949 the interior mirror changed to this rectangular shape. Deluxe models were polished.

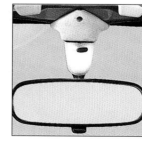

1967

This was the last year that the familiar three-screw mounting was used for the rear-view mirror.

1968

Plastic-coated surround now featured a safety-release mounting, designed to break free in an accident.

1979

The last of the cabriolets came with this somewhat ungainly combined mirror and interior light unit.

TURN SIGNALS

From the days of the earliest prototypes, the People's Car had been fitted with turn signals of one form or another, the VW30 having them incorporated into the front quarter panels, ahead of the doors. When the KdF-Wagen was launched, it appeared with semaphore signals in the door "B" pillars. It was not until 1956 that flashing turn signals first appeared, and then only on the US market. It was in the 1960s that European models were so equipped.

1975

Plain steel wheels, often fitted with accessory trims, continued in use until the '90s. Diameter remained 15in.

1938

The semaphores on this example were housed in separate boxes mounted on the front quarter panel.

1943

Type 82E used separate turn signals, despite the earlier KdF-Wagen being seen with pillar-mounted semaphores.

1948

The first pillar-mounted semaphores were made in left- and right-hand configurations.

1951

Later semaphores were not sided. Until the 1952 model, all semaphores came with grooved covers, like this.

1962

With the phasing out of semaphores for 1961 models, all Beetles featured these fender-mounted signals.

1966

From October 1963 the front turn signal was increased in size to meet new laws. The design lasted for many years.

1975

In August 1974 the front turn signals were relocated in the front bumper, making them vulnerable to damage.

REAR-VIEW MIRRORS

Many people believe the design of the Beetle never changed since the days of the KdF-Wagen. How wrong they are, for even seemingly minor components, such as the rear-view mirror, were constantly modified in an effort to improve the overall product. To begin with, the mirrors were very small, reflecting the design of the tiny split rear windows. Later, as the rear window increased in size, so did the mirrors. Cabriolets always featured dual-height mirrors.

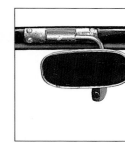

1938

The VW38 was equipped with this ellipsoidal mirror, commonly referred to as a "football" mirror.

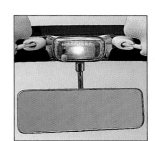

1938

The cabriolet featured a pivoting mirror which allowed the driver a view over the folded top.

1953

In October 1952 the mirror grew in size and became more rounded, echoing the new oval rear window.

1956

Cabriolets continued to use a pivoting mirror, although the design was changed in October 1952 to that shown.

1959

The 1958 model, with its new, larger rear window, saw the introduction of another new mirror design.

1962

Although padded sun visors required a modified mounting, the basic design of the mirror was unchanged.

1966

Prior to 1965, the interior mirror incorporated the sun visor mountings. Now they were mounted on the body.

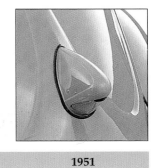

1966

The cabriolet mirror incorporated the interior light in a compact design. Note sun visor clips.

LICENSE-PLATE LIGHTS

Another seemingly insignificant detail is the light which illuminates the rear license plate on the Beetle. The design of this relatively modest component changed several times over the years, its form reflecting the gradually evolving shape of the Beetle. In the early days of the Volkswagen, the license-plate light incorporated the brake light function, making it difficult for following drivers to see when the VW was slowing down.

1938

The two VW38 Beetles in the VW Museum are fitted with this simple, round combined brake/license-plate light.

1943

The Type 82E was equipped with this unusual beak-like license-plate light housing. Brake light is included.

1944

Type 166 Schwimmwagen came fitted with this combined convoy light and license-plate illumination.

1944

The Kübelwagen had a small light mounted directly onto the deck lid to illuminate the license plate.

1951

Called a "Pope's Nose" because of its profile, this design also incorporated the brake light function.

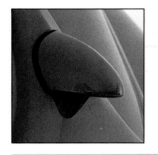

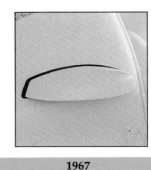

1953	1957	1959	1966	1967	1968

With the introduction of new rear light assemblies in October 1952, the license-plate light was redesigned.

Between March 1955 and August 1957, another design was used. It was more rounded than previously.

For the 1958 models, another new light was installed, which was mounted slightly higher up the deck lid.

First seen late in 1963, this wider, more angular design gave a whole new look to the back end of a Beetle.

Although superficially the same, the light unit fitted to 1967 models was new, due to the redesigned deck lid.

A redesigned, shorter and more bulbous deck lid required another minor alteration to the light unit.

DASHBOARDS

Nobody could ever accuse the Volkswagen Beetle of being a luxurious car. As soon as you sit behind the wheel, it becomes obvious from the design of the dashboard of most models that this was a vehicle built down to a price. However, this is not to suggest that the Beetle's dashboard lacks style for, regardless of year (with the possible exception of those vehicles built in the mid- to late-1970's), there has always been a certain timeless simplicity which makes it so endearing to its owners. The VW designers certainly knew what they were doing: who else could have made a painted steel dashboard look so appealing? With minimal instrumentation providing all the necessary information, what more could a Volkswagen driver possibly need?

1938	1943	1944

The VW38 set the style for Beetle dashboards for the next 14 years. The simple two-pod design housed the speedometer on the left. A gear-shift pattern appeared to its right.

Little change here except for the KdF logo blanking plate to the right of the speedometer. Note the two open glove boxes on either side of the dashboard and the minimal controls.

The Type 166 Schwimmwagen was a different matter altogether, offering no home comforts. Note the extra control levers on the floor to engage the all-terrain gear and/or the propeller.

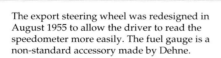
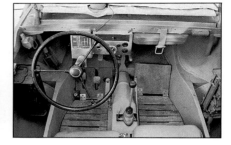

1953	1956	1959	1962

In October 1952 the dashboard was completely redesigned, with an asymmetrical layout reflecting whether the car was left- or right-hand drive. Note export steering wheel.

The export steering wheel was redesigned in August 1955 to allow the driver to read the speedometer more easily. The fuel gauge is a non-standard accessory made by Dehne.

From August 1957, the Beetle began to evolve at a greater rate than ever before, with a new rear window and a totally redesigned dashboard. Note the absence of a fuel gauge.

A new steering wheel, with chromed horn ring, was first seen in August 1960. The fuel gauge came a year later, on export models. Standard models retained the old fuel tap.

1967	1968	1974	1975

To improve safety and to help reduce reflections on the windshield, the control knobs on the dashboard were made of soft black plastic. The ashtray lost its pull knob.

Three air vents on the top of the dashboard help demisting. A new speedometer now includes the fuel gauge, while the control knobs carry symbols to aid recognition.

The biggest revision ever came with the curved windshield 1303 models. The new dashboard was of molded plastic and housed the speedometer in a raised binnacle.

The basic 1200 models retained the old-style dashboard, by now covered with black plastic padding for safety reasons. Note the basic, black two-spoke steering wheel.

1974

Despite other changes made to the deck lid of the 1303 model, the license-plate unit remained unchanged.

1975

In a cost-cutting exercise, the light unit was molded from plastic but featured styling grooves on the top surface.

1979

The last Beetles to be built in Germany, the cabriolet models, all featured this same license-plate light.

1944

The Type 82 Kübelwagen was no less austere than its military stablemate. The dashboard housed a speedometer, the electrical switch-gear and a pair of fuse-boxes.

1948

Post-war versions of the Beetle looked little different to the last of the pre-war prototypes. Note VW logo in place of original KdF marking and the simple three-spoke wheel.

1966

In an effort to help combat the perennial problem of the windshield misting up, VW added an extra air vent to the center of the Beetle's dashboard in August 1965.

1978

With the exception of the 1303-based cabriolets, the last of the German Beetles continued to use the early-style dashboard layout. Note the new-style steering wheel.

ENGINES

One of the principal reasons behind the Beetle's success was the engine: an air-cooled, horizontally-opposed four-cylinder unit mounted at the rear of the car. Designed to be a low-revving unit which, without water, could neither freeze nor boil, the VW engine soon earned itself an enviable reputation for reliability. In wartime, even when subjected to all manner of abuse from heavy-footed military personnel, the little gem of a motor kept on going. Today, some 50 years after its original appearance, the air-cooled flat-four soldiers on, powering the latest South American-built Beetles, although by now boasting such refinement as hydraulic lifters and fuel-injection. No other engine in history has been so successful.

1938

The first 985cc flat-four engine produced a modest 24bhp at just 3,000rpm. Note the single, centrally-mounted carburetor and long inlet manifold. Generator is belt-driven.

1943

An increase to 1131cc in early 1943 resulted in a small power increase to 31hp at 3,300rpm. Cooling fan is driven from generator shaft and is located within the fan housing.

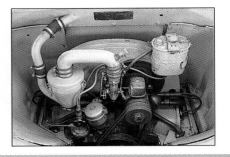

1944

The Type 166 Schwimmwagen engine was identical to the regular Beetle engine of the time. Drive to rear-mounted propeller was taken from the end of the crankshaft.

1948

Lever on top right of fan housing allowed owner to set cooling system to summer or winter positions. Note "coffee tin" air-filter – now a highly-prized item among restorers.

1953

Although engine remained at 1131cc, a new oil-bath air-filter and revised cooling system helped to make the engine more efficient and reliable. Carburetor is Solex 28PCI.

1956

Engine size was increased to 1192cc in December 1953. This resulted in a power output of 36hp at 3,700rpm. The increase in capacity was due to a larger cylinder bore.

1962

All-new 1192cc engine was introduced in August 1960, with a power output of 40hp at 3,600rpm. So-called "non-fresh air" heating system remained essentially as before.

1967

The 1493cc ("1500") engine was first used in the Type 2 models. Recognized as being one of the finest engines built by VW, the new unit produced 53hp at 4,000rpm.

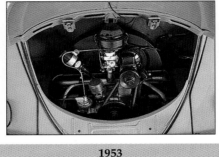

1968

The 1300 engine continued to be offered alongside the 1200 and 1500 units but, in common with VW policy, was constantly upgraded. Note new air-filter design.

1974

First seen in 1971, the 1584cc engine featured new cylinder heads with dual inlet ports. Producing 57hp at 4,000rpm, the engine was the most powerful yet offered in a Beetle.

1975

The 1192cc engine remained in production but had, by now, seen many detail revisions, including the fitment of a more efficient alternator charging system.

1978

In Germany, the last of the saloon models produced at Emden differed little mechanically from those built over the previous 10 years. Sadly, the end was in sight.

1979

To meet strict anti-emission laws in the USA, Volkswagen fitted a Bosch AFC fuel-injection system on certain models. A catalytic convertor in the exhaust cleaned up emissions.

1944

Type 82 Kübelwagen was also powered by the same 1131cc engine. The air filter was designed to allow engine to breath in dusty conditions. Note excellent engine access.

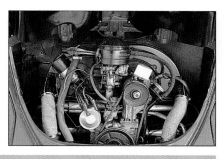

1966

An increase in engine size to 1285cc resulted in a power output of 50hp at 4,000rpm. As with all engines built from July 1962, a new "fresh air" heating system was used.

Porsche Project Numbers Relating to Volkswagen

Every project which was undertaken by the Porsche design office was allocated a number. Many of these projects never reached fruition, being little more than design exercises.

60 KdF Beetle Project
61 Scaled-Down Beetle
62 Cross-Country VW
64 Record Attempt VW
65 Driving School VW
66 Right-Hand Drive VW
67 Invalid Carriage
68 VW Van
81 Parcel Van Chassis
82 Cross-Country VW
83 Automatic Gearbox
84 Twin-Clutch Gearbox
85 4-Wheel-Drive VW
86 4-Wheel-Drive Cross-Country VW
87 4-Wheel-Drive based on Type 82
88 VW Van
89 Automatic Gearbox
92 Type 82 Chassis with KdF Bodywork
98 Type 128 with KdF Bodywork
106 Experimental Gearbox
107 Turbocharger
115 Supercharged Engine
120 Stationary Engine for Air Force
121 Stationary Engine for Army
122 Stationary Engine for Post Office
126 Synchromesh Gearbox
127 Sleeve Valve Engine
128 Amphibious Vehicle
129 Amphibious Vehicle
132 Containers
133 Carburetor
138 Amphibious Vehicle
151 Experimental Gearbox
152 Experimental Gearbox
155 Snow Track for Type 82
156 Railroad Conversion for Type 166
157 Railroad Conversion for Type 82
160 Unitary Construction VW
162 Cross-Country VW – Unitary Construction
164 6-Wheel Light VW – Twin Engines
166 Motorized Infantry VW
172 Containers
174 Assault Boat Engine
177 5-Speed Gearbox
178 5-Speed Gearbox
179 Fuel-Injected Engine
182 2-Wheel-Drive Cross-Country VW – Unitary Construction
187 4-Wheel-Drive Cross-Country VW – Unitary Construction
188 4-Wheel-Drive Amphibious VW
225 Experimental Gearbox
227 4-Wheel-Drive Components
230 VW with Gas Generator
231 Acetylene-Powered VW
235 Electrically-Powered VW
237 VW Engine
238 VW-Powered Winch
239 VW with Wood-Gas Generator
240 Gas-Powered VW
247 VW Aero Engine
252 Gearbox
274 Spring-Action Starter
276 Type 82 with Towing Hook
278 Synchromesh Gearbox
283 Type 82 with Gas Generator
287 Kommandeurwagen Chassis
296 Gearbox
307 Carburetor
309 Diesel Engine
330 VW with Combination Wood-Coal System
331 VW with "Native" Fuel system
332 Anthracite-Powered VW

Type Numbers Used by VW Under British Control (1945-48)

While under the control of the British Army, the numbering system used by the factory was revised, bringing it in line with the reduced number of vehicles which were to be built.

11 Beetle Sedan
13 With Sliding Roof
15 Two-Seater Cabriolet
21 Kübelwagen
25 Fire Tender
27 Open Van
28 Closed Van
51 Beetle with Type 82 Chassis
53 With Sliding Roof
55 Cabriolet with Type 82 Chassis
81 Pick-Up
83 Panel Van
91 Open Trailer
93 Closed Trailer
100 Short-Wheelbase Beetle

Volkswagen Type Numbers (1949 to Present)

A new Type number had to be allocated to every new model launched. The following is a complete list of numbers relating to all air-cooled Volkswagens produced in Germany.

111 Standard Beetle Sedan (LHD)
112 Standard Beetle Sedan (RHD)
113 Export Beetle Sedan (LHD)
114 Export Beetle Sedan (RHD)
115 Standard Beetle Sedan, sliding roof (LHD)
116 Standard Beetle Sedan, sliding roof (RHD)
117 Export Beetle Sedan, sliding roof (LHD)
118 Export Beetle Sedan, sliding roof (RHD)
141 Hebmüller 2-Seat Cabriolet (LHD)*
141 Karmann Ghia Cabriolet (LHD)*
142 Karmann Ghia Cabriolet (RHD)
143 Karmann Ghia Coupé (LHD)
144 Karmann Ghia Coupé (RHD)
151 Beetle Cabriolet (LHD)
152 Beetle Cabriolet (RHD)
181 Trekker ("Thing")
211 Van – door on right (LHD)
213 Van – door on right (LHD)
214 Van – door on left (RHD)
215 Van – doors on both sides (LHD)
216 Van – doors on both sides (RHD)
221 Microbus – door on right (LHD)
223 Microbus – door on right (LHD)
224 Microbus – door on left (RHD)
225 Microbus – doors on both sides (LHD)
226 Microbus – doors on both sides (RHD)
231 Kombi – door on right (LHD)
233 Kombi – door on left (LHD)
234 Kombi – door on left (RHD)
235 Kombi – door on right, sliding roof (LHD)
237 Kombi – door on left, sliding roof (LHD)
238 Kombi – door on left, sliding roof (RHD)
241 Microbus De Luxe (LHD)
244 Microbus De Luxe (RHD)
251 Microbus De Luxe – 7-seater (LHD)
261 Pick-Up – side-panel on right (LHD)
263 Pick-Up – side-panel on left (LHD)
264 Pick-Up – side-panel on left (RHD)
265 Double Cab Pick-Up – door on right (LHD)
267 Double Cab Pick-Up – door on left (LHD)
268 Double Cab Pick-Up – door on left (RHD)
271 Ambulance – door on right (LHD)
273 Ambulance – door on left (LHD)
274 Ambulance – door on left (RHD)

281 Microbus – 7-seater – door on right (LHD)

285 Microbus – 7-seater – door on right, sliding roof (LHD)

311 Fastback (LHD)

312 Fastback (RHD)

313 Fastback, sliding roof (LHD)

314 Fastback, sliding roof (RHD)

315 Notchback (LHD)

316 Notchback (RHD)

317 Notchback, sliding roof (LHD)

318 Notchback, sliding roof (RHD)

361 Variant (LHD)

362 Variant (RHD)

363 Variant, sliding roof (LHD)

364 Variant, sliding roof (RHD)

365 Variant "A" (LHD)

366 Variant "A" (RHD)

367 Variant "A", sliding roof (LHD)

368 Variant "A", sliding roof (RHD)

343 Type 3 Karmann Ghia (LHD)

344 Type 3 Karmann Ghia (RHD)

345 Type 3 Karmann Ghia, sliding roof (LHD)

346 Type 3 Karmann Ghia, sliding roof (RHD)

411 2-Door Sedan "L" (LHD)

412 2-Door Sedan "L" (RHD)

415 2-Door Sedan (LHD)

416 2-Door Sedan (RHD)

421 4-Door Sedan "L" (LHD)

422 4-Door Sedan "L" (RHD)

425 4-Door Sedan (LHD)

426 4-Door Sedan (RHD)

461 Variant "L" (LHD)

462 Variant "L" (RHD)

465 Variant (LHD)

466 Variant (RHD)

(* NB: Duplicated Type Number)

Volkswagen Production Figures (1945-1980)

The Beetle broke all production records during its lifetime. As can be seen, until as late as 1974, the Beetle accounted for the majority of worldwide Volkswagen production.

Year	Beetle	Total VW
1945	1,785	1,785
1946	10,020	10,020
1947	8,987	8,987
1948	19,244	19,244
1949	46,146	46,154
1950	81,979	90,038
1951	93,709	105,712
1952	114,348	136,013
1953	151,323	179,740
1954	202,174	242,373
1955	279,986	329,893
1956	333,190	395,690
1957	380,561	472,554
1958	451,526	557,088
1959	575,407	705,243
1960	739,443	890,673
1961	827,850	1,007,113
1962	876,255	1,184,675
1963	838,488	1,209,591
1964	948,370	1,410,715
1965	1,090,863	1,542,654
1966	1,080,165	1,583,239
1967	925,787	1,300,761
1968	1,136,134	1,707,402
1969	1,219,314	1,830,018
1970	1,196,099	1,989,422
1971	1,291,612	2,071,533
1972	1,220,686	1,895,192
1973	1,206,018	1,927,809
1974	791,053	1,778,738
1975	441,116	1,649,895
1976	383,277	1,862,711
1977	258,634	1,806,750
1978	271,673	1,439,000
1979	253,340	1,397,000
1980	236,177	–

Beetle Chassis Numbers 1945-1979

The chassis numbering system was changed in 1957 when the new model year was deemed to start on August 1st each year. Numbers shown represent last unit for given month.

Year	July	December
1945		1-053 814
1946		1-063 796
1947		1-072 743
1948		1-091 921
1949		1-138 554
1950		1-220 133
1951		1-313 829
1952		1-428 156
1953		1-579 682
1954		1-781 884
1955		1 060 929
1956		1 394 119
1957	1 600 440	1 774 680
1958	2 020 302	2 226 206
1959	2 528 282	2 801 613
1960	3 204 566	3 551 044
1961	4 010 994	4 400 051
1962	4 854 999	5 225 042
1963	5 677 118	6 016 120
1964	6 502 399	115 410 000
1965	115 979 202	116 463 103
1966	116 1021 298	117 422 503
1967	117 844 902	118 431 603
1968	118 1016 098	119 474 780
1969	119 1093 704	110 2473 153
1970	110 3097 089	111 2427 591
1971	111 3143 119	112 2427 792
1972	112 2961 362	113 2438 833
1973	113 3021 911	114 2423 795
1974	114 2828 457	115 2143 743
1975	115 2266 092	116 2071 467
1976	116 2176 287	117 2063 700
1977	117 2096 890	118 2026 312
1978	–	119 2108 687
1979	119 2121 136	11A 008 929
1980	11A 0020 000	–

INDEX